Together as Brothers

A History of the Brothers of St. Pius X

Diocese of La Crosse, WI

By

Brother Michael Mandernach

With Richard Berendes and Rose Peterson

This silhouette of four Brothers was taken by Father Albert Roemer on the monastery grounds in October of 1954. It won two awards from a Milwaukee newspaper and was used many times in the publication of THE PAX. It was taken on a typical fall day, with the sun setting in a partly cloudy sky. The dog accompanies the Brothers (left to right): John Resch, Edward Zimmer, Charles Bisenius and Michael Mandernach.

Printed by La Crosse Graphics Inc., La Crosse, WI

ISBN-13: 978-1-628-90001-9

ISBN-10: 1-6289-0001-6

Front and Back Cover Design by John Horsfall, a graphic artist in La Crosse, WI, where he lives with his wife and two daughters.

Images within the book are taken from THE PAX or from artwork done by individual Brothers. Pictures are courtesy of the Archives at the La Crosse Diocesan Center, many of which were taken by the first Director of the Brothers, Father Roemer.

Copies of Together as Brothers may be ordered from:
Hurley Religious Goods Store
P.O. Box 174
Fargo, ND   58107
1-800-437-4338

DEDICATION

This book is dedicated to the men who served their lives,

or a portion of their lives, as Brothers of St. Pius X,

and to the bishops, priests, fellow religious

and faithful people of God

who supported them.

ABOUT THE AUTHOR

Brother Michael Mandernach was born in St. Martin, Minnesota. He was the third of thirteen children, and one of five to join religious life. At the age of 23, and three months after the founding of the Community, Brother Michael joined the Brothers of St. Pius X, where today he is in his 60th year as a religious Brother. He is the sole surviving member of the Community.

Brother Michael embodies the word Brother. A Brother is a lay Christian man who commits himself to Christ and the Christian community by making vows of poverty, chastity and obedience. Brother Michael lives his life of prayer and witness to Christ's loving presence by his service. These past several decades have been dedicated to pastoral ministry. He is also known for his gentle kindness and charity toward all he encounters. Brother Michael is ideally suited to author this book given his remarkable recall for events and names of the people involved, as well as for his intense love for the Brothers of St. Pius X, the people they served and the men who formed community with him.

TABLE OF CONTENTS

ACKNOWLEDGEMENTS

The author acknowledges and expresses appreciation to:

His Eminence Raymond Leo Cardinal Burke, for his recommendation to write this history and for writing one of the forewords.

His Excellency Bishop William P. Callahan, OFM Conv., for his encouragement and for writing one of the forewords.

Monsignor Michael Gorman, for writing about his experience of having eight different Brothers as religious education teachers during his grade school years, and for his support and association with the Brothers, as well as for writing one of the forewords.

All former Brothers of St. Pius X, living or deceased, for their input into this history, their presence with us, and their constant support and friendship.

Father Kevin Louis, my Pastor at Sacred Heart Parish, for encouraging me to get the task completed.

Fathers Eugene Smith, Myron Meinen and William Rorke, for their assistance to Father George Passehl during the time of his directorship.

Father Robert Cook, the chaplain to the Brothers while they lived in the Trane house. He was also the paper boy for the Brothers when they lived in the 1105 King Street House in 1952.

Father John Cassidy, Pastor at Sacred Heart Parish in De Soto, and a friend to all the Brothers during our last years in De Soto.

Monsignor Matthew Malnar, for his expertise in making the document theologically sound and readable.

Carol Richards, for her expertise and diligence in repeated editing and for her sound recommendations each time to ensure that the content flowed properly.

Priests who reside at Holy Cross Diocesan Center and staff who work there, for their daily support: "How are you doing with the History?" or "Are you about finished?" Those questions kept me going through the ups and downs of writing.

THE CATHOLIC TIMES, for photos of Raymond Leo Cardinal Burke, Bishop John Paul, Archbishop Jerome Listecki, Bishop William Callahan, OFM Conv., Fathers George Passehl, Albert Raschke, Anton Lecheler, and Edward Penchi, and for the photo of the St. Pius X Coat of Arms.

Richard Berendes, for his contribution to the writing of the document, for his remembrances of many of the events that happened within the Community, and for his enthusiasm for the task.

Rose Peterson, for her knowledge of word processing, for her expertise in formatting the manuscript and her help in a thousand little ways.

The Brothers of St. Pius X collectively acknowledge and express appreciation to:

The Bishops and priests of the Diocese of La Crosse with whom we ministered for the advancement of the Kingdom of God here on earth. Let us say, "It has been a joy and a delight."

The priests of the Archdiocese of Dubuque, Iowa, the Diocese of Superior, the Archdiocese of Chicago, the Holy Cross Fathers and Brothers, the Jesuits, the Servite Fathers, the Capuchin Fathers and Brothers, the Precious Blood Fathers, the Dominicans, the Benedictines, the Trappists, and the Brothers of Christian Schools. You, too, were most kind to us. We generously thank you.

The Franciscan Sisters of Perpetual Adoration, the Benedictine Sisters of Eau Claire, the School Sisters of Notre Dame, the Franciscan Sisters of St. Joseph, the Sisters of the Sorrowful Mother, the Servite Sisters, the Sisters of Holy Cross, the School Sisters of St. Francis, the Sisters of Mercy, and the Our Lady of Victory Missionary Sisters. You were the Congregations of Sisters with whom we had the privilege to work. Thank you for the opportunity.

The dedicated and devoted lay people, with whom we shared ministries in healthcare, education, and many other professions. We say a grateful, "Thank you!"

FOREWORD

His Eminence Raymond Leo Cardinal Burke, D.D., J.C.D.

Prefect, Supreme Tribunal of the Apostolic Signatura

International Director of the Marian Catechist Apostolate

By the time I was named Bishop of La Crosse, my home diocese, on December 10, 1994, there were just two remaining members of the Brothers of Saint Pius X, a diocesan congregation of religious brothers founded in the early 1950s by one of my predecessors, Bishop John Patrick Treacy. In a certain sense, born in 1948, I can say that I grew up in the Diocese with the Brothers, since the Brothers were founded when I was four years of age. My family moved from Richland Center to Stratford in 1959, at about the same time that the Brothers established their house and farm in nearby Colby, not far from our farm in Marathon County. Entering Holy Cross Seminary in September of 1962, I had daily contact with the Brothers who served in a variety of ways the important work of the diocesan seminary. After ordination to the Holy Priesthood in 1975 and my assignment to the Cathedral of Saint Joseph the Workman, I had regular contact with the Brothers who were engaged in teaching, healthcare, and other apostolates. In 1977, in addition to my service at the Cathedral, I was assigned to teach religion at Aquinas High School where I worked closely with Brother Kevin Brutcher, the head of the religion department.

Over the years, I witnessed the growth of the membership of the Brothers and their embrace of a variety of apostolates, in accord with the needs of the Church and with the particular gifts of each Brother. Bishop Treacy had a great vision for the service of the Brothers within the Diocese of La Crosse, to which the Brothers strove faithfully to respond. Sadly, I also witnessed the decline of the membership of the Brothers in the years following the close of the Second Vatican Ecumenical Council. The confusion in the implementation of the Conciliar Decree *Perfectae Caritatis*, which addressed the fitting renewal of religious life, at a time when the Brothers were also beginning to govern themselves without the direction of a diocesan priest, naturally presented a formidable challenge for a relatively young diocesan religious congregation.

I recall, in particular, the post-Conciliar confusion about the distinct vocation of the religious Brother and the conviction among many that men called to the religious life should all be priests. To be frank, having witnessed the Brothers living their vocation with so much fidelity and generosity, I was always offended by the implication that somehow the vocation of the religious Brother did not have its own integrity, and was not its own distinct gift from the Holy Spirit for the building up of the life of the Church. In the renewal after the Council, it seems that one of the important principles regarding the richness of the vocation to the consecrated life, namely respect for the integrity of the distinct grace of the Holy Spirit given for the foundation of the various institutes of consecrated life, was either overlooked or deliberately set aside. *Perfectae Caritatis* enunciated the principle with these words:

It redounds to the good of the Church that institutes have their own particular characteristics and works. Therefore let their founders' spirit and special aims they set before them as well as their sound traditions – all of which make up the patrimony of each institute – be faithfully held in honor.[1]

This principle both respects the theological reality of each foundation and, at the same time, safeguards it against a worldly pragmatism which views religious men and women as mere employees and religious institutes as mere providers of workers for the Church.

In the specific treatment of religious institutes devoted to the apostolate, the Council once again enunciated the important principle of respect for the distinct work of the Holy Spirit in each religious institute. In noting the many communities, including lay, that is non-clerical, communities like the Brothers of Saint Pius X, the Council called to mind the importance of respect for the integrity of the gift of grace given to each community for the good of the whole Church. The Council ordered the fitting renewal of apostolic religious communities with these words:

> There are in the Church very many communities, both clerical and lay, which devote themselves to various apostolic tasks. The gifts which these communities possess differ according to the grace which is allotted to them…
>
> These communities, then, should adjust their rules and customs to fit the demands of the apostolate to which they are dedicated. The fact however that apostolic religious life takes on many forms requires that its adaptation and renewal take account of this

---

[1] "In ipsum Ecclesiae bonum cedit ut instituta peculiarem suam indolem ac munus habeant. Ideo fideliter agnoscantur et serventur Fundatorum spiritus propriaque proposita, necnon sanae traditiones, quae omnia cuiusque instituti patrimonium constituunt." Sacrosanctum Concilium Oecumenicum Vaticanum II, Decretum *Perfectae caritatis*, "De accommodata renovatione vitae religiosae," 28 Octobris 1965, *Acta Apostolicae Sedis* 58 (1966), 703, n. 2b. [Hereafter, *PC*]. English translation: *The Documents of Vatican II with Notes and Index*, Vatican Translation (Strathfield, NSW: St Pauls Publications, 2009), p. 274, no. 2b. [Hereafter, *PCEng*].

diversity and provide that the lives of religious dedicated to the service of Christ in these various communities be sustained by special provisions appropriate to each.[2]

While the Council ordered the adjustment of "rules and customs" according to the apostolates to which communities of apostolic religious are dedicated, at the same time, it first ordered respect for the distinct gift of the Holy Spirit in each institute of consecrated life, a gift which is the source of the love of Christ and of His Mystical Body, the Church, expressed by means of the apostolate.

In various conversations with Brother Michael, he mentioned to me that the Bishop, priests, other consecrated persons and lay faithful had, at different times, suggested to him that he should study to be a priest. I could understand their suggestion because Brother Michael provided excellent assistance to the priests in the various parishes in which he served. In a pragmatic way, given his gifts, one could ask why Brother Michael did not present himself to study for the priesthood. Brother Michael's response was simple: God called him to be a religious Brother, not a priest, and, therefore, he found joy and peace in living faithfully his proper vocation. Knowing Brother Michael over many decades, I have never doubted that he was following God's call fully, and I understood that he never felt the need to follow a call other than that to which he had first responded in 1952 when he entered the community of the Brothers of Saint Pius X.

---

[2] "Permulta sunt in Ecclesia instituta, vel clericalia vel laicalia, variis apostolatus operibus dedita, quae donationes habent secundum gratiam quae data est eis, differentes: …
Quapropter instituta illa observantias suas atque usus cum requisitis apostolatus, cui dedicantur, apte componant. Cum autem vita religiosa apostolicis operibus dedita formas multiplices induat, necesse est ut accommodata eius renovatio huiusmodi diversitatis rationem habeat, atque ut apud varia instituta sodalium vita in servitium Christi propriis eorum congruisque mediis sustentetur." *PC*, 706, n. 8. English translation: *PCEng*, p. 277, no. 8.

During my years of service as a priest of the Diocese of La Crosse and most especially as Bishop of La Crosse, regular communication with the two remaining Brothers, Brother Michael and Brother Charles Bisenius, was always a source of inspiration and encouragement to me. They were among the first to join Bishop Treacy's new religious foundation in 1952 and remained always for me a living sign of all that the Brothers of Saint Pius X have meant for the Diocese of La Crosse. Since Brother Charles frequently was living and serving outside of the Diocese of La Crosse, and, by the time I became Bishop, had retired to his family home in Cascade, Iowa, I had less contact with him. Nevertheless, he was always faithful in keeping in communicating with me and visiting with me, whenever possible. His death on March 14, 2012, left Brother Michael as the sole surviving Brother.

Brother Michael, because of his enduring fidelity to his vocation as a religious Brother and because of his dedication to the service of the Diocese of La Crosse, to which he had come from the Diocese of Saint Cloud in Minnesota to enter the Brothers of Saint Pius X, accepted and carried out with generosity a variety of important missions. To put it simply, the Bishop and priests of the Diocese of La Crosse could always count upon Brother Michael. He is a most worthy representative of the great gift of the Brothers of Saint Pius X to the Diocese of La Crosse and to the wider Church in which they have also served. Brother Michael, in fact, continues to live faithfully and generously his vocation, as he has done now for some sixty years.

One of my goals as Bishop of La Crosse was to provide more appropriately for the Diocesan Archive and thereby to make possible and encourage the serious study of the history of the Diocese. The concern to know and appreciate the history of the Church is simply an expression of our

Catholic faith, which teaches us that God the Son took our human nature and, entering history, took a human heart, in order to heal our hearts of sin and to fill them with His own pure and selfless love. We know that Christ, who suffered, died, and rose from the dead, is now seated in glory at the right hand of the Father, from which He unceasingly pours forth, from His glorious pierced Heart, the sevenfold gift of the Holy Spirit, healing us of sin and strengthening us to love God and our neighbor. Christ is alive for us in the Church. The study of the Church's history helps to understand how Christ continues to act for our eternal salvation and to see how we may become ever more perfect co-workers with Him.

Because of my concern for a complete and accurate history of the Diocese of La Crosse, early in my time as Bishop I asked Brother Michael to write the history of the Brothers of Saint Pius X. Although, at the time, Brother Charles and he were in good health, I knew that the time had come for Brother Michael, who had lived the history of the Brothers practically from their first days, to begin the substantial work of making a record of all that he and his confreres had experienced. Brother Michael, with his characteristic good will and diligence, immediately began the work which, thanks be to God, he has now brought to a good conclusion. Over the years, he has kept me informed of his progress. I can honestly say that I never doubted that he would complete well this work asked of him by the Church whom he loves so deeply and to whom he has consecrated his life.

The work of writing the history turned out to be more challenging than I had imagined. When I asked Brother Michael to provide an important chapter of the history of the Diocese of La Crosse, I imagined that, in addition to his complete and rich experience of the life of the Brothers of Saint Pius X from their first year, he would find many helpful documents in the Archive of the Diocese, especially the documents regarding the foundation of the Brothers, the vision of the founder, Bishop Treacy, and their spiritual patrimony. The sad truth is that he found very little, a fact which I am unable to explain fully. Certainly, there had been less than adequate provision for the Archive of the Diocese. Also, from time to time, it seems those who had the responsibility for the careful preservation of the documents of the Church in the Diocese did not fully understand the importance of certain papers and, therefore, discarded them as useless. The situation may have been aggravated by the false conclusion that, since the Brothers of Saint Pius X were declining in numbers, the documentation regarding them was no longer of practical importance.

The late Father Gerald E. Fisher, in his history of the Diocese of La Crosse, written on the occasion of the centennial of the founding of the Diocese, offers a brief commentary on the foundation of the Brothers of Saint Pius X by Bishop Treacy.[3] Since he does not note any references for his commentary, one suspects that it is based on his direct experience, having been ordained a priest of the Diocese in 1951 and having taught civics and history in the Diocesan seminary for many years. Although he claims that "the immediate reason for launching a brotherhood" was Bishop Treacy's thought "that a diocesan order would be especially useful in maintenance work at Holy Cross [Seminary]," he ultimately attributes the foundation of the Brothers to the vision of Bishop Treacy for the apostolate of Catholic education in the Diocese, with these words:

> Bishop Treacy thought of the future of the vast diocesan education
> program, and considered that certain posts, for example, coaches,
> administrators, teachers, and maintenance men might well be filled

---

[3] Cf. Gerald Edward Fisher, *Dusk Is My Dawn: The First Hundred Years, Diocese of La Crosse, 1868-1968* (La Crosse, WI: Allied Printing, 1969), p. 145. [Hereafter, *Dusk Is My Dawn*].

by brothers.[4]

Reading the history of the relationship of Bishop Treacy with the Brothers, as Brother Michael recounts it, it seems fair to say that the bigger vision of a religious institute dedicated to the apostolate of Catholic education was in the Bishop's mind from the beginning, even if he may also have thought that the Brothers could provide a number of important services at the Seminary which he rightly considered the heart of the Diocese. In fact, from the early days of the Brothers, they were intimately associated with the catechetical and educational apostolates of the Church.

Writing in 1968, Father Fisher noted that the Brothers "are now seventeen years old and are vigorously anticipating a flourishing apostolate in the spirit of Vatican II."[5] He even expressed the thought that the Brothers "might well be the 'dark horse' of [Bishop Treacy's] multifaceted legacy."[6] Father Fisher expresses a certain euphoria, prevalent in the late 1960s, regarding the renewal of Church life mandated by the Council. Interestingly, he uses the term, "spirit of Vatican II," which sadly was not always appropriately tethered to the careful study of the teaching of the Council. As I noted above, dealing with the confusion generated by the "spirit of Vatican II" was a most difficult challenge for so young a religious congregation. Father Fisher's thought regarding the place of the Brothers of Saint Pius X in the "multifaceted legacy" of Bishop Treacy was not realized as perhaps he imagined. In another sense, however, the Brothers of Saint Pius X remain historically an important part of the life of the Church in the Diocese of La Crosse and, therefore, the legacy of Bishop Treacy.

The lack of documents in the Diocesan Archive and the rather brief and

---

[4] *Dusk Is My Dawn*, p. 145.
[5] *Dusk Is My Dawn*, p. 145.
[6] *Dusk Is My Dawn*, p. 145.

undocumented treatment in the official history of the Diocese did not discourage Brother Michael. He simply worked with greater diligence to supply for what he should have been able to discover in the Diocesan Archive or other official records of Diocesan history. Having read carefully the entire manuscript of his work, I believe that he has recorded, in as complete a manner as possible, the story of the Brothers of Saint Pius X as a particular manifestation of the life of Christ in the Church in the Diocese of La Crosse. Even though he has lived practically the entire history of the Brothers, Brother Michael also was careful to seek the assistance of others who had been his confreres, especially Mr. Richard Berendes, in writing the history.

Humanly speaking, one could consider the history of the Brothers of Saint Pius X to be a mere record of past events of a religious institute with one sole surviving member. In the eyes of the Church, however, it is a record of the Holy Spirit at work in the Brothers for the glory of God and the salvation of souls. Brother Michael's history consistently underlines the abiding heritage of the Brothers. In that sense, as I noted above, the Brothers are a proud and lasting part of Bishop Treacy "multifaceted legacy." I underline just a few of the notable aspects of Brother Michael's history which illustrate that heritage.

The font of the vocation of the religious brother is his personal encounter with Christ through daily prayer and, most of all, through the Sacred Liturgy. From the very beginning, daily participation in the Holy Mass and the praying of the Liturgy of the Hours held the primacy of place for the Brothers of Saint Pius X. It is striking to note that the men who spent time with the Brothers and then returned to the world all express the deepest gratitude for the discipline of prayer and love of the Sacred Liturgy which continued to sustain them.

A personal recollection of mine has to do with the manner in which the Brothers informed their farming activity with the Sacred Liturgy. The processions on the occasion of the Rogation Days were a beautiful expression of the essential importance of the Sacred Liturgy for farmers as stewards of the plants and animals for the sake of us all. The farmer is blessed to work with God in a most intimate way in providing for the good of His children. For that reason, the Sacred Liturgy sustains the farmer in carrying out his irreplaceable service with integrity. The Brothers of Saint Pius X, over the years when they maintained farms at De Soto and Colby, reflected very much the historical unity of the Liturgical Movement and the Catholic Rural Life Movement. In our time, farming has suffered from the effects of what is called 'vertical integration"; it has become big business. The Brothers of Saint Pius X were powerful witnesses to the truth about farming as a privileged cooperation with God in His care of the earth and, above all, of His sons and daughters whom He has created in His own image and likeness, and whom He has redeemed by the Redemptive Incarnation of His only-begotten Son.

Another reflection of the heritage of the Brothers is the strong sense of the common life, an essential characteristic of religious life, with which they lived their vocation. When I was Bishop of La Crosse, I was privileged to celebrate in 1999 a reunion of all who were or had been Brothers of Saint Pius X and, in August of 2002, to offer the Holy Mass on the occasion of the fiftieth anniversary of the foundation of the Brothers. On both occasions, I was deeply moved to observe the lasting bond among those who had been members of the Brothers of Saint Pius X.

Striking also is the manner in which Brother Michael writes about all those whom he came to know as confreres. His respectful and loving appreciation of each member of the Brothers manifests the strength of the common life, which by nature marks the life of every religious institute. I recall the words of *Perfectae Caritatis* about the common life:

Common life, fashioned on the model of the early Church where the body of believers was united in heart and soul (cf. Acts 4:32), and given new force by the teaching of the Gospel, the sacred liturgy and especially the Eucharist, should continue to be lived in prayer and the communion of the same spirit. As members of Christ living together as brothers, religious should give pride of place in esteem to each other (cf. Rom. 12:10) and bear each other's burdens (cf. Gal. 6:2).[7]

Certainly the Brothers, like any community of human beings, experienced their moments of irritation and disagreement with each other, but what they clearly experienced much more strongly was their communion with each other in the single-hearted service of Christ their Brother. Even the title which Brother Michael chose to give to his history of the Brothers, *Together as Brothers*, underlines the common life as a quality which marks strongly the entire history.

In conclusion, it remains only to express my heartfelt esteem and gratitude to Brother Michael Mandernach for a work well done. *Together as Brothers* is a worthy record of the action of the Holy Spirit in the community of the Brothers of Saint Pius X. It is an account told with the truth and love of one who, from his youth and now for some 60 years, has cooperated faithfully and generously with the Holy Spirit in response to the call to the

---

[7] "Vita in communi agenda, ad exemplum primaevae Ecclesiae in qua multitudo credentium erat cor unum et anima una (cfr. *Act.* 4, 32), evangelica doctrina, Sacra Liturgia et praesertim Eucharistia refecta, in oratione et communione eiusdem spiritus perseveret (cfr. *Act.* 2, 42). Religiosi, ut membra Christi, in fraterna conversatione honore se invicem praeveniant (cfr. *Rom.* 12, 10), alter alterius onera portantes (cfr. *Gal.* 6, 2)." PC, 709, n. 15. English translation: *PCEng*, p. 281, no. 15.

apostolic religious life as a Brother. As a native son of the Diocese of La Crosse, who was deeply honored to be a priest of the Diocese of La Crosse and to be its Bishop, I offer heartfelt gratitude to Brother Michael for the steadfastness with which he worked on the history of the Brothers of Saint Pius X, since that day in 1996 when I first asked him to provide for the Diocese and for the Church a written record of this important chapter of her history.

Lastly, in my own name and in the name of all the faithful who have known the Brothers of Saint Pius X over the years since 1952, I thank the Brothers and ask that God grant them the reward of their faithful and generous dedication to the religious life of lay Brothers. In a particular way, I thank Brother Michael for his fidelity and generosity. Knowing Brother Michael has been one of the special graces which God has granted to me in my life. I thank God for Brother Michael and ask that God continue to bless him abundantly and to bless, in a particular way, this, his latest work, the history of his religious institute, *Together as Brothers*.

Raymond Leo Cardinal BURKE
Prefect of the Supreme Tribunal of the Apostolic Signatura
21 April 2014 – Easter Monday

FOREWORD

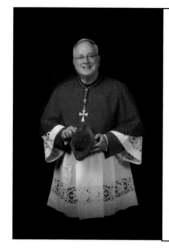

Bishop William Patrick Callahan, OFM Conv.

Diocese of La Crosse, Wisconsin

DIOCESE of LA CROSSE

✝

Office of the Bishop

In a time when authentic religious community is so highly prized – especially among young people in the world – it seems quite appropriate that a new book relating the history and ministerial activities of a small, but spiritually powerful group of Religious Brothers, founded in the heartland of America, should make its appearance in our lives. This book tells the story of the Brothers of Pius X. While none other than one of the original Community remains alive at the time of this publication, the story and legacy is offered to inspire the next generation of pioneers into the fields of the Lord that are rich and ready for the harvest.

The motto of the Brothers' patron, St. Pope Pius X, was adopted as a philosophy and model of life for the Community, namely: "Restore all things in Christ." With that insight and the theological and practical zeal of the saintly pope, the brothers' community extended itself into the life of the Church and the specific works of the Diocese of La Crosse, Wisconsin.

The elements of evangelization that are at the forefront of the Church, empowered by the insights of <u>Lumen Gentium</u> and <u>Gaudium et Spes,</u> became the structure of the Brothers' community life and apostolic ministry. These two foundational documents from the Second Vatican Council became the centerpiece of the action plan that spoke to the urgency of restoration and renewal for all people in Christ, thus assisting and empowering the Brothers in their own work for Christ's Church.

As you explore the history of the Brothers of Pius X in these pages, I sincerely hope that the legacy of their lives and the service they offered the Church will inspire you and lead you to the fuller expression of Christ's mission in your own life.

(signature) † William Patrick Callahan

Most Reverend William Patrick Callahan, OFM Conv.

Diocese of La Crosse, Wisconsin

Solemnity of the Immaculate Conception, 2013

FOREWORD

Monsignor Michael J. Gorman

Vicar General and Moderator of the Curia

Diocese of La Crosse, Wisconsin

The Brothers of Saint Pius X were the catechists in my home parish of Saint Philip near Rolling Ground, Wisconsin, and that is how I've known them. I had at least eight of them as catechists and over the years I have known quite a few more of them. Brother Michael Mandernach, the author of this history, was my first-grade catechism teacher. I thought it was neat that we had the same name. Catechism class in those days was a half day on Saturday morning consisting of an hour of class, recess, another 45 minutes of class, music practice in church and Mass. Then we had two weeks of summer school after school got out which were full days. It was a good program and provided a sound doctrinal foundation to which I often referred back during my years in the seminary (the 1970s) when the teaching being offered was not always faithful to Catholic tradition. I believe my catechetical formation had given me a good-enough understanding to be able to sort out what was authentic theology and what was speculation.

The Brothers also had an impact on my vocational discernment. First of all they were men whom I admired and thought of emulating. I also was intrigued by the black cassock and green scapular they wore as their habit. When I was in the fifth grade I was trained to be a Mass server by Brother Kevin Gordon, who is now a priest in the Diocese of Superior. When I was in the sixth or seventh grade the Brothers held a vocation day at De Soto. Among the materials I picked up that day was a prayer which I said every day from then on until I was ordained. It began, "Lord Jesus, what do you want of me? Would you have me one day standing at the altar as your priest?" It is a prayer that I later had made into a bookmark prayer card by our diocesan Vocations Office and used to distribute to the servers when I was the Master of Ceremonies for Bishop John Paul and then-Bishop Raymond Burke. I have since learned that a number of those servers said that prayer, and some became seminarians and even priests.

I have found this history of the Brothers of Saint Pius X to be interesting reading. The first reason is because I have known many of the brothers and priests mentioned within. The second reason is to know something of the ethos of the community. The struggles and poverty they endured were never evident to us who had them as catechists. They were totally dedicated to their ministry and were men of the Church. They certainly enhanced my knowledge and appreciation of the Catholic faith and I am glad to have known them both as teachers and as friends.

PREFACE

On August 15, 1996 I had a meeting with Bishop Raymond Leo Burke, the Bishop of La Crosse, Wisconsin at that time. I met him at his residence, since it was the Feast of the Assumption of Mary, and the Diocesan Offices were not open that day. When we finished discussing the matter for which I came, he said with a smile on his face, "I think someone should write the history of the Brothers of St. Pius X." He looked at me, waiting for a response. Now, there were only Brother Charles and I left, and I knew he was aware of that. Slowly, I answered, "Well, if it needs to be done, I'm probably the one to do it. But do you think anyone will read it?" He encouraged me to take on the project and to write at least something to put into the diocesan archives.

One of the reasons why it came to then-Bishop Burke's mind to write the history of the Brothers was that, in checking the diocesan files for information about the Brothers, he found very little. I knew that Father Albert Roemer, our first Director, and Bishop John Treacy had communicated a great deal with personal visits and by letter. I knew, because I had typed a lot of their letters myself. Bishop Burke then apologized, having realized that someone must have mistakenly discarded some of the files pertaining to the Brothers.

The writing of this history is basically the work of all the men who were ever members of the Brothers of St. Pius X. The information gathered comes from the 1954 to 1977 issues of our monthly publication, THE PAX, from files in the Congregation's records (minutes of our Council meetings, our General Chapter's deliberations), and from responses to the questionnaires I sent out, as well as from discussions with former Brothers. I coordinated this material to formulate a story describing the presence of the Brothers of St. Pius X in the Diocese of La Crosse for the short period of their existence. Contained within this history is a listing of the men who joined, although a few men who stayed only a very brief time are not included. I wish to credit all these Brothers as part of this history. In THE PAX, the names of the writers of most articles are not given. Many of the Brothers contributed their thoughts and ideas. I acknowledge their contributions.

The stories of "Benny the Bee" and "Barney" were written by Father Roemer. The Director's Column in THE PAX was written by Fathers Roemer, Passehl and Raschke, and later by Brothers Kevin Brutcher, Conrad Henninger and me. I use many of their thoughts and quote some in this history.

Our Congregation has now been in existence for over 60 years. There are many aspects of our history that are not included. I tried to cover the highlights as I read them and remembered them. My purpose in writing this history, and I think Cardinal Burke would agree, is to provide a glimpse of who we were, and a description of our prayer life, our apostolate and areas of ministry, as well as what paths of life former members entered.

This history of the Brothers of St. Pius X reflects my experience and time with the Brothers, which included all but the first three and one-half months. For the last 61 years, I have been a member, and I have tried to live the Community's spirit.

With the help of Richard Berendes, who shared his experiences and that of other members by means of a questionnaire and discussion, I have written this document to give you a sense of our lives as religious Brothers. Other former members who entered after the Congregation had been established would have an altogether different view. They would not have dug trenches, cut firewood, used an outdoor biffy and hauled rocks. Neither would they have experienced learning together how to pray the Breviary and how to build a chapel.

At the 60th anniversary celebration in August, 2012, I told the group of former Brothers that I would be finishing the Congregation's history, and I asked for their input. All of them agreed that it should be finished; all were willing to give their input through a questionnaire which I was to formulate. Their responses to the questionnaire are included. Richard Berendes volunteered his help, and that has been tremendous.

It is my hope that, if you met any of the Brothers of St. Pius X, you would have felt that you met a man of God, a man of prayer, a man who saw God in you, and a man you could call your Brother in Christ.

1   Beginning

"How good and how delightful it is for all to live together as brothers," begins *Psalm* 133. Was this beautiful verse in the mind and heart of Bishop John Patrick Treacy, STD, Bishop of La Crosse, as he pondered the beginning of a diocesan religious congregation of Brothers? He had just completed many building projects in the Diocese, one of which was the magnificent Holy Cross Seminary in 1951, located in a beautiful setting on the south side of La Crosse on the banks of the Mississippi River. Three hundred seminarians occupied the institution, as well as a rector and a full teaching staff.

Bishop Treacy had also built several new Catholic high schools in the Diocese and numerous grade schools. He was proud of the Catholic educational program as well as all the other church-related activities which were going on throughout the nineteen counties that comprised the Diocese. The Bishop, however, was concerned about the staffing of these schools and institutions.

One day in October of 1951, he found out that two of his seminarians were leaving Holy Cross Seminary to join religious communities which had Brothers. Both of these young men, Donald McAllister and Marcus Resch, were eighteen years of age and were in their first year of college. Both were from Wausau, Wisconsin. Mark was from St. James Parish and Donald from St. Anne's.

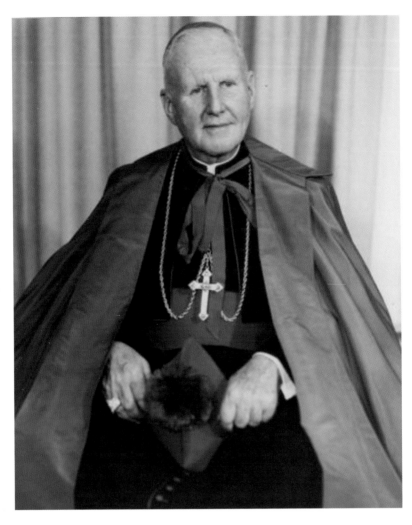

Bishop John P. Treacy, Founder of the Brothers of Pius X

Earlier, Donald McAllister had talked with Father Floyd Dwyer, the Spiritual Director at the Seminary, about the possibility of a Diocesan Brotherhood. Donald envisioned a community of Brothers who would be teachers in the Catholic Schools of the Diocese, nurses in the various hospitals and health care centers, catechists, parish ministers and who would serve in many other positions in the apostolate. Donald was interested in the vocation of religious brother. Marcus, too, thought that he had a calling to the brotherhood.

As Bishop Treacy thought about these two young men, he must have discussed it with his Chancellor, Monsignor George Hammes, his secretary, Father James Finucan, and probably a few other priests of the Diocese.

Certainly, Father Dwyer would have mentioned to Bishop Treacy the conversation he had had with Donald McAllister. The question arose: What was the possibility of these two young men serving in the Diocese? If they were interested in religious life, what could he as Bishop do to enable these men to become religious and yet serve in the Diocese? Bishop Treacy was familiar with some of the religious communities serving in the Diocese: the Jesuits at St. Gabriel's Parish and Campion High School in Prairie du Chien, the Capuchins at St. Anthony's Friary in Marathon and the Sacred Heart Fathers and Brothers in Sparta. He knew full well the talents and gifts of the men of these religious orders and the great service they provided the Diocese. It was widely known also that, even though Bishop Treacy greatly admired and respected these religious orders, he believed that most parishes in the Diocese should be served by diocesan priests. He wanted all of the young men from the Diocese to serve in the Diocese, especially if they were interested in the priesthood or Brotherhood.

Now Bishop Treacy was faced with these two young men thinking about joining religious orders that most likely would lead them to areas of ministry and service outside the Diocese. Through much presumed prayer for guidance from the Holy Spirit and discussion with diocesan advisors, the idea of establishing a Diocesan Brotherhood emerged as a possibility. Would Donald and Mark be interested if a congregation of diocesan brothers were established? What would the clergy of the Diocese think about this venture? Would they be supportive of this endeavor? After all, the priests were already financially stretched to the limit in their parishes with the cost of the new Seminary and other institutions that had been established within the last few years.

This was the fall of 1951, and the financial burden of the Diocese was increasing. Another institution, especially a Diocesan Brotherhood, might be looked upon as another one of Bishop Treacy's dreams. Some of the priests believed that enough institutions had been initiated and that some time should be allowed before any more buildings or institutions were begun. Bishop Treacy was used to the fact that not everyone agreed with his hopes and dreams, but this did not deter him from proceeding with any project he felt would strengthen the Church in the Diocese of La Crosse. One of his favorite sayings was, "The Diocese of La Crosse is second to none." Or, as the inscription on the front door of the gymnasium of the Seminary stated, "It is better to aim high and miss than to aim low and hit." Bishop Treacy had high goals and expectations of himself and all those around him. He had a great vision for the people of the Diocese of La Crosse.

Some of the priests who were active in ministry at that time mentioned that the idea of a Diocesan Brotherhood did not receive overwhelming approval from the clergy of the Diocese. Some surmised that it was just one of Bishop Treacy's wild dreams, and others felt that a Diocesan Brotherhood was not really needed. After all, there were many religious Sisters in the Diocese who carried out much of the educational and catechetical ministries. The Brothers of Christian Schools were teaching at Pacelli High School in Stevens Point and McDonnell High School in Chippewa Falls. So what was the big deal about a new Diocesan Brotherhood?

However, this did not stop Bishop Treacy from doing what he felt the Holy Spirit was calling him to do. He decided to begin a Diocesan Brotherhood for the Diocese of La Crosse. Many questions remained to be answered. What was to be the name of this new brotherhood? Who would be its first Director? Where would they live? What type of spiritual formation would they be given? What would be their apostolate? What Rule and Constitutions would they follow? How would Donald and Marcus be contacted and asked if they were interested in joining this new religious Brotherhood? These were just a few of the questions facing Bishop Treacy, and face them he did, one by one.

One of the first things the Bishop did was to call Monsignor Thomas O'Shaughnessy, pastor of St. James, and Father Philip Leinfelder of St. Anne's, both in Wausau, to ask them to contact Marcus and Donald to share the idea of a Diocesan Brotherhood with them. Then they were to ask if the two young men would be interested in being the first members of the Congregation. Marcus and Donald agreed. The two pastors took them to La Crosse on November 27, 1951. They met with Bishop Treacy, who shared with them his ideas of what this new brotherhood might be. Marcus and Donald began working at the Chancery, while residing at St. Michael's Home, a residence for children without parents. The Bishop promised that he would soon appoint a Director. There was excitement about the new Community's foundation and its expectations.

First Director: Father Albert P. Roemer

On November 27, the priests of the Diocese met in a clergy conference at which the new Diocesan Brotherhood was announced. There was much discussion about the Brotherhood among the priests; many of them kidded

4

one another that they might be the new Congregation's first Director. Father Albert P. Roemer was at the conference and later wrote in his diary: "The Bishop said that the Spiritual Director would be appointed. A thought came to me: 'What a fine thing it would be,' and immediately the thought was dismissed with just a little feeling of disappointment." Father Roemer went on to write about how some of the priests joked with him that he would be asked to direct the Brothers, especially his close personal friend, Monsignor C. W. Gille. (Monsignor Gille already knew that Father Roemer would be asked.)

Father Roemer prepared for his return to St. Alexander's Parish in Port Edwards, where he served as pastor. Just as he stepped into his car, a priest told him that the Bishop wanted to see him. Thinking that the priest was joking, he proceeded to start his car, at which time Monsignor Gille pleaded for him to stop, which he did. Then Father Roemer went to see the Bishop. The Bishop asked him if he was interested in becoming the first Director and spiritual advisor for the newly-established Diocesan Brotherhood. He explained to Father Roemer the possibilities for this new religious congregation in the Diocese, and as the Bishop spoke, Father Roemer's heart warmed toward the proposal. Soon Father Roemer accepted the invitation. In his letter of acceptance on November 30, 1951, he mentioned his enthusiasm about the Diocesan Brotherhood, stating, "I want to give everything to it. I realize that the weaker the instrument, the more the work may be the work of God."

Why did Bishop Treacy select Father Roemer as the first Director? In the fall of 1951, he could have chosen from many talented and gifted priests. There seemed to have been two qualities in Father Roemer which led the Bishop to select him:

1)   Bishop Treacy saw in Father Roemer a priest whose spirituality was focused on Jesus in the Gospels, a spirituality that he manifested in a joyful way. Father Roemer's infectious laugh, his magical tricks and his ability to make people around him happy showed his love of people in such a way that everyone in his presence felt special. His spirituality and his ministry and person as a priest were united.

2)   Father Roemer had Brothers as teachers in high school. He had some understanding of the vocation of "Brother." He understood the call to the priesthood as a call from God. His experience with the Christian Brothers helped him to understand that the call to

become a Brother was also a call from God. It seemed that the Bishop felt that Father Roemer possessed the gentleness, as well as the firmness that was needed, to deal with all circumstances which might arise in a new Community of Brothers.

Father Albert P. Roemer, First Director of the Brothers of Pius X

Father Roemer was born in Wilmette, Illinois. He was ordained for the Diocese of La Crosse on June 7, 1941. He was assistant pastor at St. Joseph's in Baraboo and St. John's in Marshfield before becoming pastor of St. James in Rising Sun, with St. Mary's in Viroqua as its mission. In 1947, he became the Diocesan Director of the Confraternity of Christian Doctrine and wrote a weekly column, "The Guiding Light," for the Diocesan Catholic paper. In 1950, Father Roemer became pastor of St. Alexander's in Port Edwards. He was very much in demand for directing high school retreats and Cana Conferences, as well as preaching at Forty Hours Devotion services.

In his younger days Father Roemer was a member of the Chicago North Shore Boxing Team. Perhaps that was one of the determining factors in his selection as Director of young men in a religious community of Brothers! Father Roemer, who was known as one of the great preachers of the Diocese, could instill within the Brothers the necessary training required of religious in the Church then. One of the priests who knew him said that Father Roemer loved to go to other parishes and other states to preach Forty Hours Devotions and retreats. Bishop Treacy felt that if he appointed Father Roemer as Director of the Brothers, he would not be able to continue to travel but that Father Roemer's gifts would be used to form the men who would become Brothers. Bishop Treacy wanted to use Father Roemer's talents in a diocesan setting.

Selecting a Name

What was this new Brotherhood to be called? Bishop Treacy discussed it with Father Roemer and other priests. The Bishop wanted some reference to the Blessed Sacrament because of his devotion to the Eucharist; he felt that the celebration of the Eucharist should be at the heart and soul of every religious congregation. He knew of the Congregation of the Blessed Sacrament, founded by St. Peter Julian Eymard. The Bishop expressed his wish that the name should have a certain modern reference to it. In a discussion one day, it was mentioned that Blessed Pope Pius X had given children the privilege of receiving Communion at the age of reason, whereas previously, the age had been around twelve. It was at this time that the name of Blessed Pius X came up for discussion; soon, it was agreed that the new Diocesan Brotherhood would be called "Brothers of Blessed Pius X." Blessed Pius X would be an ideal model for men living the life of religious Brothers. The Community ideal would be "to restore all things in Christ," the motto of Pope Pius X's papacy.

Giuseppe Melchiorre Sarto – Pope Pius X

Giuseppe Melchiorre Sarto was born on June 1, 1835, the second child of ten born to Giovanni and Margharita Sarto in Riese on the Venetian Plain in Italy. Giovanni was the *cursore* of Riese, a sort of town clerk and assistant to the mayor. His mother had been a dressmaker before she married. In addition to Giovanni's work as *cursore*, the family farmed a little over two acres. They inherited the house they lived in, which was better than a peasant's cottage but definitely not middle class. Giuseppe was born into a hard-working poor family, one with a simple yet powerful faith that God would always provide. As Giuseppe grew, he became "Beppo" to his parents, siblings, friends and, eventually, to some of his parishioners.

Saint Pius X, Patron of the Brothers of Pius X

At the age of eleven, Giuseppe entered the College of Castelfranco, which was about four miles from Riese. He walked to and from the College every day and frequently went barefoot, his shoes tied around his neck, to save his family the expense of shoes. In his last year at Castelfranco, Giuseppe expressed a desire to become a priest. At the time, families of seminarians were expected to bear the cost of their priestly education and formation, and the Sarto family could not afford the financial burden. Even though the family had little money, his mother especially trusted in Divine Providence. If their son was to be a priest, somehow or other, the money would come. In view of Beppo's academic record and vocational disposition, the prefect of studies at Trevisio Seminary, Canon Casagrande, approached the Patriarch of Venice, Cardinal Marco, to see if something could be done. Providentially, Cardinal Marco, happened to come from Riese himself, and soon a "free place" was arranged for Beppo at the Seminary of Padua by means of a letter from the Cardinal dated August 22, 1850.

Beppo's father died soon after he entered the seminary. At times, Beppo felt as if he was needed to help support the family, but his mother advised him to continue to study for the priesthood. He was ordained on September 18, 1858, with all the people of Riese rejoicing. He went through the usual steps of a priest becoming an assistant pastor and shortly after, a pastor. He was ordained a Bishop in 1884. On the evening of the day he was ordained Bishop, Beppo showed his episcopal ring, of which he was very proud, to his mother. His mother greatly admired his ring and told him how beautiful it was. Then, with a smile on her face, she pointed to her wedding ring and said, "You wouldn't have your ring if it wasn't for this ring." He was assigned to the Diocese of Mantua.

On June 12, 1892, Bishop Sarto was made a Cardinal at a public Consistory. He was promoted to the Patriarchate of Venice a month later. It was at Venice that his spirit of piety as a pastor and Bishop became known to all. He had a great love for Gregorian Chant, the "true song of the Church," words which he so often used. From Venice he went to the Conclave on July 26, 1901, to help elect a successor to Pope Leo XIII, who had died on July 20. As Cardinal Sarto was leaving for Rome, one lady startled him by saying, "Your Eminence, I am asking the Holy Spirit to make you Pope!" Cardinal Sarto turned to her with a smile, "All I can say is that you certainly have a funny idea of the Holy Spirit." When he left for the station, a great shout of farewell went up. "Safe journey! Go in health! Come back to us!" From the fleet of gondolas all along the Grand Canal arose greetings and prayers; from the little bridge men and women leaned

9

down to him, waving and saying, "Come back to us!" It was a refrain constantly growing in volume. As his gondola went down the canal, a huge concourse of boats fell in behind him.

There was already a crowd waiting at the train station. When the fleet of gondolas pulled in behind the Cardinal's, he was encircled by the crowd. They touched his cape, cried and laughed. The Cardinal was overwhelmed by the time he arrived at the steps of the waiting train; he could hardly speak. Yet, the hand of his people seemed to be reaching for his heart. "Come back! Come back to us!" The Cardinal turned at last. His face was as radiant as a sunrise on an April morning. "I promise to return," he said gravely. "Dead or alive, I will return to my people!" he exclaimed.

The Conclave to elect a successor to Pope Leo XIII began in 1901. When Cardinal Sarto received five votes on the first ballot, he told the Cardinal next to him, "The Cardinals are having a little joke at my expense." After balloting he went to the Pauline Chapel to pray. At the second ballot, he received twenty-one votes. It now became clear to him what he never thought might happen. It was unbelievable. "Please," he begged the Cardinals, "don't vote for me. I am unworthy, incapable of filling this great office. Please forget me." Again, he went to the Chapel to pray.

Cardinal Sarto's friend, Cardinal Merry de Val, was sent to ask him if he would accept, if elected. He found Cardinal Sarto in prayer. Cardinal Merry del Val knelt down beside him. Cardinal Sarto raised his head, and Cardinal Merry de Val saw his tear-stained face. To observe Cardinal Sarto at close quarters was to love the man. His charm was indefinable. The quickness of his mind and his witty conversation were impressive. His radiance made him stand out above all others. His humanity and deep spirit of prayer spoke volumes. When Cardinal Sarto left the Chapel, a number of Cardinals came to ask him to accept.

When finally he spoke, it was with a child's simplicity. "But how can I accept?" he asked. "I'm unworthy, far too unworthy. And I made a solemn promise to my people that I would return to them. I swore that I would return to Venice dead or alive." Finally Cardinal Sarto responded to the three Cardinals who persisted, saying, "I must accept the will of God." In the evening ballot, Cardinal Sarto received thirty-five votes. The next morning, he received fifty-five votes, eight more than the number required. As he heard his name repeated over and over by the tellers, his whole body trembled with emotion. At the conclusion of the count, he rose and prostrated himself before the papal altar. When asked if he accepted,

Cardinal Sarto raised his head, and the Cardinals present heard his clear voice, "If this chalice cannot pass from me, the will of God be done. I accept." He chose the name Pius.

When Cardinal Sarto stepped on the train in Santa Lucia Station on July 26, 1901, he had no idea he would not return to Venice as Giuseppe Sarto. He also could have had no understanding of the grander acts set in motion by this train ride, least of all, the birth, fifty years later, of a humble Catholic Brotherhood in a small town in Wisconsin on the banks of the mighty Mississippi River.

What a wonderful model Blessed Pius X would be for Bishop Treacy's Diocesan Brotherhood. As Pope, so many of his accomplishments and gifts became known to the whole world. His motto, "to restore all things in Christ," became the foundation of his whole pontificate. "May God in His mercy hasten the restoration of the whole human race to Jesus Christ" were words in his first encyclical.

Other achievements, such as the codification of Church law, the proper instruction of the faithful through the revised Catechism, regulation of Church music through his Motu Proprio, frequent and daily Communion, his confrontation of Modernism, his love for the Bishops and priests of the world, and his great sensitivity and respect for all people, as well as his other virtues, made him an excellent patron. Bishop Treacy was most pleased to choose Blessed Pius X as the patron for the "Brothers of Blessed Pius X."

First Home for the Brothers of Blessed Pius X:

1105 King Street, La Crosse

Where would the Brothers live? Since all the seminarians now lived in the new Holy Cross Seminary building, one of the homes formerly used to house seminarians was available. It was located at 1105 King Street. Bishop Treacy called Father Roemer and mentioned that he had a place for the Brothers to live, and that he would like Father Roemer to come to La Crosse on January 5, 1952. The Bishop had wanted to give Father Roemer three months to study religious orders, but that was no longer possible because he wanted the official date for the foundation of the Brothers of Blessed Pius X to be January 6, the Feast of the Epiphany. Word spread at St. Alexander's Parish in Port Edwards that their pastor, Father Roemer, had been appointed as Director of the Brothers and was to leave Port Edwards. The people quickly arranged a farewell for him. It was at this farewell that Mr. and Mrs. Carl Schiebler gave Father Roemer $100 for the Brothers. This was the first gift to the Brotherhood.

First Home: 1105 King Street, La Crosse, Wisconsin

Father Roemer met Marcus and Donald, and they talked about all the possibilities of the new Brotherhood. All three of them were excited and anxious to begin. Donald and Marcus knew about the 1105 King Street house since they had both lived in it while seminarians. It was, however, Father Roemer's first visit. The house had been empty for a few months and seemed cold and forbidding. Donald and Mark began sanding floors and cleaning things up. Father Roemer's headquarters were at the Michael Mitchell residence in the next block while the house was readied. Mr. Mitchell was a wonderful Irishman and friend, who put Father Roemer in touch with "the right people" in La Crosse. Monsignor Alphonse Schuh, the director of St. Michael's Home, gave the Brothers some beds and furniture. The people of St. Alexander's Parish in Port Edwards also collected furniture that was picked up on January 16.

On January 26, an altar was set up in one of the rooms. Mass was celebrated for the first time on that date. What an overwhelming experience it was for the three! It was the beginning of many liturgical celebrations in the years to come. The same evening, after all the necessary items were collected, the men had their first Holy Hour. It became a regular practice in the life of the Brothers to have both daily Mass and an evening Holy Hour with Exposition of the Blessed Sacrament. It was at the conclusion of the Holy Hour, with only a light on the statue of the Blessed Mother, that the Salve Regina was sung. It closed their day, followed by Grand Silence until after breakfast the next day.

The announcement of the new Diocesan Brotherhood was printed in most of the Catholic diocesan newspapers throughout the country, and many young men wrote for information. On January 27, Father Roemer gave a Cana Conference in Pittsville, Wisconsin, accompanied by Donald and Marcus. A young man by the name of William Kundert approached Father Roemer, asking if he could join. He was accepted and arrived on February 5.

Now that the house was beginning to look great, Father Roemer decided to invite Bishop Treacy to come for a formal opening of the house and to bless it. January 31 was set aside for this celebration. Bishop Treacy came for Mass and blessed the house. Fathers Thomas Mullen, William Mooney, Hugo Koehler, Henry Hoerburger, James Finucan and other priests attended. It was at this celebration that Bishop Treacy shared with all the desire of placing the Brotherhood under the patronage of Blessed Pius X. He stated that the thought came to him amidst a distraction while making his meditation one day. Father Roemer told him that he thought his distractions were very worthwhile. All present agreed again that Blessed Pius X was an excellent choice.

A great helper to the Brothers in this initial stage was Monsignor Alphonse Schuh. He visited often, brought meat from St. Michael's Home, and took Father Roemer to meet the local merchants. Monsignor Schuh would often let the candidates use the jeep to haul items. Gertrude Lemmeier, Bishop Treacy's housekeeper, visited and admired the progress that had been made on the house.

Father Roemer and the candidates sat down to plan a daily schedule. A morning Mass and an evening Holy Hour were to be part of every day. Discussion began about the possibility of having a Breviary of some kind. Of course, each day also contained work time to accomplish what needed to be done.

Father Roemer was asked to give a series of eight radio broadcasts in Sparta. After these broadcasts, Father Leroy Keegan gave him a donation of

$200.00. It was at this time that Bishop Treacy asked Father Roemer if the Brothers could become self-supporting. The Chancery financed the Brothers for the first two months, but because of the overwhelming financial burden on the Diocese due to the building of the Seminary and other diocesan institutions, the Brothers were to be financially independent. Since Father Roemer was writing a weekly column in the diocesan Catholic paper, he asked for contributions. Father Roemer contributed the check for $200.00 to the Brothers and, for the next ten years, he gave all of his finances and earnings to help finance the Brotherhood.

On February 4, Francis Peters came from West Bend, Wisconsin for an interview. He was a brother to Father Raymond Peters of the Diocese of La Crosse. Francis came to stay on March 4. He was the fourth official candidate.

Father Roemer and the first four candidates: L to R: Marcus Resch, Fr. Roemer, William Kundert, Francis Peters, Donald McAllister

Selecting a Religious Habit

What kind of a religious habit would the Brothers wear? In that day, most members of religious communities wore some kind of distinctive garb that immediately identified them. Bishop Treacy felt the Brothers should also have a garb that would identify them. Father Roemer contacted Mr. Chick Holland of Crawfordville, Indiana, a designer by trade. The Bishop had expressed a desire to have a black cassock and some kind of a scapular with an emblem. Working out the details was left to Father Roemer and the candidates. On March 15, 1952 Mr. Holland came to meet with Bishop Treacy and Father Roemer. He came up with the idea that the scapular should be green. It did not appeal to Father Roemer at first, but he slowly came to like it. Father Roemer's idea was that the emblem on the scapular should be a Eucharistic design because Blessed Pius X was pre-eminently the Pope of the Eucharist. He urged frequent Holy Communion in the modern world and made it possible for children to receive Communion upon reaching the age of reason. Mr. Holland recommended that Blessed Pius X was also known as the *Pope of Peace*, and some of his last words were, "I give my life for peace." Mr. Holland wanted the emblem to contain the word "PAX." Father Roemer mentioned that this would be very fitting since peace is a direct fruit of the Eucharist and also because the world was dreadfully in need of peace, both for individuals and for society.

Bishop Treacy had to leave the first meeting early, and so another meeting was scheduled with him. What would he think of these ideas? After some preliminary remarks, the Bishop asked about the habit. Mr. Holland explained to him the idea of the green scapular. The Bishop's face registered definite disapproval, probably because he thought people would say he selected green because of his Irish heritage. The Bishop asked Father Roemer his opinion about the green. Father Roemer agreed that it would seem rather unusual to have a black cassock with a green scapular, but he also mentioned that Our Lady gave the green scapular to a humble nun in Paris, expressing her desire for devotion to her Immaculate Heart. Mary declared to the nun that it would bear fruit in the return of lapsed Catholics and difficult conversions. The Bishop's face lit up at the mention of this. Green was also the color of hope and the spiritual growth and peace that come from hope. Fathers Hammes and Finucan were called in for their opinions. Startled at first, they agreed with everyone else that the green scapular should be chosen as part of the habit of the Brothers of Blessed Pius X.

Father Roemer thought a Eucharistic emblem should be considered, but Mr. Holland strongly felt that the word "PAX" with the Chi-Rho symbol would be more appropriate for the Brothers of Blessed Pius X. All ideas and sketches were submitted to Sister Patrice, FSPA of the Viterbo College Art Department. She drew a beautiful six-sided black emblem with "PAX" written through the Chi-Rho in green. It was placed in the front at the center of the scapular. Everyone involved with that matter agreed on this design and it became the habit of the Brothers. Concerning the habit, Father Alfred Hebert, then rector of Holy Cross Seminary, kidded Father Roemer, "Every religious order has miracles in its beginning. I see nothing miraculous in the origin of the Brothers of Blessed Pius X, certainly not in its first director, but there is one miracle! It is the habit!"

Brothers in habit: L to R (back row): Brothers Thomas, Mark, Francis

L to R (front row): Brothers Michael, Charles, John, Anthony

On May 13 the habits arrived. Everyone was quite pleased with them. On May 17, the candidates were invited to Father Urban Baer's parish in Eastman for Confirmation. They brought the habits along, and Donald put one on for the Bishop and the priests to see. The "oohs" and "aahs" indicated that everyone was pleased.

16

Community at Prayer

Brothers in the King Street Chapel

The Holy Week services in 1952 were celebrated in the tiny chapel on King Street, but for the Tenebrae and other Easter services the Brothers went to St. Joseph's Cathedral, where they also attended the Solemn Pontifical Easter Mass.

"With gratitude in your hearts sing psalms and hymns and inspired songs to God" (*Colossians* 3:16). Every religious order or congregation strives to develop a strong prayer life in its members as well as a community. On April 14, 1952 the Brothers began chanting the whole Roman Breviary in English. Father Roemer thought of using an abbreviated version, but the candidates decided that the whole Breviary would be more meaningful. Probably, the Brothers of Blessed Pius X were one of the first communities of Brothers in the Church to pray the Breviary in the vernacular. It took a while for them to learn where to go in the four-volume system and, every once in a while, they were on the wrong page or in the wrong lesson. Father Roemer, who prayed it in Latin in those days, would steer them back on the right path.

A New Candidate

Wilfred Mandernach (Brother Michael, the author) entered the scene on April 25, immediately becoming the senior member at age twenty-three. Marcus, Donald, Bill and Francis were all eighteen and nineteen. Wilfred arrived in La Crosse by bus about 6:00 p.m. from St. Martin, Minnesota. He took a taxi to 1105 King Street. He asked the taxi cab driver, "Are you sure this is 1105 King Street?" "Yes," the driver said, and drove away. Marcus answered the door and welcomed Wilfred. He then met Donald, Bill and Francis. Father Roemer was gone for the evening and met Wilfred the next morning. Now there were five candidates.

The Gift of De Soto

Father Roemer received a letter from Bishop Treacy saying, in effect, "If you pray right, I think you could obtain a farm where you can grow and develop as God intends." Wow! The message kept running through Father Roemer's mind. He decided to begin a novena of Holy Hours to Blessed Pius X for this intention. On the ninth day of the novena, Father Roemer was preaching for a Forty Hours Devotion in Eastman. The priests who attended the Devotion bantered with Father Roemer about a farm.

A few people were mentioned as possible donors. Finally, Father John McMahon of Bangor, Wisconsin, formerly of Rising Sun and De Soto, spoke of a Mrs. Anna Loftus of De Soto, who had a farm, as a prospective donor. Father Roemer arranged with Father McMahon to go to see her. She had just had a heart attack and was convalescing. It was May 21, just at the close of the novena. Father Duffy joined the two priests, and Mrs. Loftus was most gracious in her welcome. Father McMahon became the spokesperson.

"I'm going to make you the happiest woman in the world," he said in his winning way.

'You are?" Mrs. Loftus said questioningly. "How?"

"We're going to put the new Congregation of Brothers right over in your house across the street!" stated Father McMahon.

"You are! Well, that's wonderful," said Mrs. Loftus.

"The Brothers will be able to support themselves here," said Father McMahon.

'How will they be able to do that?" asked Mrs. Loftus.

"Why, on the land!" said Father.

"And who will give them the land?" questioned Mrs. Loftus.

"Why, you will," responded Father McMahon.

Mrs. Loftus then explained that she did not own the property but that it belonged to her son, Richard Paul, an attorney in New York City. She agreed to write to him immediately.

Anna Loftus and her son, Richard P. Loftus

Father Roemer and the five candidates anxiously waited for a reply. Soon it came. Mr. Richard Loftus said that he was delighted to give the property to the Brothers. It consisted of two houses, a barn, some machine sheds, and two hundred acres of wooded bluffs with about an acre of tillable land. Mr. Loftus stated that nothing had made him quite as happy as being able to donate the property that would become the home of the Brothers of Blessed Pius X.

On June 5, Bishop Treacy and Fathers McMahon, Finucan and Roemer drove to De Soto to see Mrs. Loftus. She was again immensely pleased to see the Bishop and priests. She was a delightful lady, quite elderly, and very vivacious for her age. All of them posed for pictures, and the Bishop told her that when the transactions were completed, the photos would appear in the *La Crosse Register*. Mrs. Loftus told them about the interesting history of Sacred Heart Church in De Soto which was located next to the Loftus property. The rock for the structure of the church was quarried on the Loftus property in 1891. Mrs. Loftus also shared how the children of the parish came to her house for catechetical instructions some years back. All were pleased with the day.

The First Investiture

Time was drawing near for the investiture ceremony for the candidates. Father Roemer prepared a ceremonial for the occasion. He consulted with the Brothers of Mary from Galesville as well as the Franciscan Sisters of Perpetual Adoration in La Crosse. Especially significant for the ceremony was the prayer Father wrote for the bestowal of the green scapular:

> Receive, O most beloved Brother, this green scapular. May you now wear it for the glory of God in honor of the Blessed Virgin Mary and Blessed Pius X, so that having the protection of the same Virgin and Pontiff, you may live justly, charitably, joyfully, and with great confidence in the goodness of the Heart of Jesus, and at the hour of death come to eternal glory. Amen.

Many other details for the ceremony needed attention: music, homilist, programs, reception and invitations. The ceremony was to be celebrated at St. Joseph's Cathedral in La Crosse on June 20, 1952. Monsignor Peter Pape, the rector, was most gracious in helping to make all of the arrangements.

Donald, Marcus, Bill, Francis, and Wilfred (later, Michael) went to the Trappist Monastery near Dubuque for retreat in preparation for the investiture. Since Wilfred had only arrived two months earlier, he did not become part of the first group. All of them were deeply inspired with the monastic spirit of the monastery. Father Michael, OCSO gave the retreat. His knowledge of Scripture overwhelmed the candidates as he spoke of the message of Jesus found in the Gospels. The Trappists chanted the Divine Office with such reverence and prayerfulness. It was a splendid retreat. Especially impressive to the candidates on the retreat was meeting Brother Joachim, the porter for the monastery. His wonderful and kindly concern had a powerful influence by way of example. His courtesy, his smile, his self-forgetfulness and the saintliness which radiated from him will always be remembered. The Brothers were told that an image of his face was once used in a magazine most closely representing the face of Jesus. We could see why.

The investiture ceremony was celebrated at St. Joseph's Cathedral with close to one hundred priests and family members of the candidates present. Bishop Treacy thanked them kindly for being present and for their interest in the Brotherhood. Bishop William Mulloy of Convington, Kentucky had given a recent priest retreat and was also present for the ceremony. Father Roemer was the celebrant for the Mass, with Bishop Treacy bestowing the religious habits to the four candidates. Father John McMahon gave the homily entitled "Fools for God."

Bishop Treacy told the congregation about the donation of the De Soto property to the Brothers by Richard Loftus and mentioned that his mother, Anna Loftus, was present for the celebration. The Bishop lauded the Loftus family for their spirit and their generosity.

The four candidates took the following names as religious:

Donald McAllister	Brother Thomas
Marcus Resch	Brother John
William Kundert	Brother Joseph
Francis Peters	Brother Francis

First Investiture Ceremony on June 20, 1952

Brothers Joseph, Thomas, John and Francis

St. Joseph's Cathedral in La Crosse, Wisconsin

De Soto, Wisconsin – Here Come the Brothers!

It was moving time, and it was time to begin packing. Brother John had asked his brother Tony for a truck, and on July 4 the Brothers moved everything they had to De Soto. Much of it was old furniture, but they took everything. Mr. and Mrs. Joseph Ghelfi had been living in the main house, and so they moved to the smaller house next to Mr. and Mrs. Carl Prell. This opened the main house for the Community. What a sight! There was furniture on the lawn, suitcases on the porch and utensils in every room. First the Brothers had to move all of the Loftus furniture to the sheds before theirs could be moved in. With everything rather chaotic, the Brothers decided to have a picnic. It was already 3:00 p.m. They had wonderful steaks - tube steaks, that is - wieners!

How delighted and pleased the Brothers were to have their own place. It provided space and they were close to the mighty Mississippi River. The beauty of the bluffs, the many green trees and the view of the River truly gave them a sense of the beauty of God and His creation. *Psalm* 148 expressed their feelings very well:

Alleluia! Let heaven praise God, praise Him, heavenly heights,

Praise Him, all His angels, praise Him, all His armies!

Praise Him, sun and moon, praise Him shining stars,

Praise Him, highest heavens, and waters above the heavens! . . .

Let earth praise Yahweh, seas, monsters, and all the deeps,

Fire and hail, snow and mist, gales that obey His decrees,

Mountains and hills, orchards and forests,

·Wild animals and farm animals, snakes and birds . . .

This psalm grew in meaning since the Brothers could see all of this beauty from their chapel window. One could be overwhelmed with this area of Wisconsin, known as "God's Country." Since every religious congregation developed a prayer life for its members, this newly-founded Community of Brothers searched for theirs.

Inside the main house were two rooms, formerly used as living rooms, where the Brothers set up their little chapel. In one room, they erected a small altar with a tabernacle and a crucifix hanging above it on the wall. In the other room, which had an arched opening, three pews were placed. Each day the Brothers would gather here for the celebration of Mass, the chanting of the Divine Office, meditation and personal prayer. They would come together as a Community seven times a day, patterning their schedule from *Psalm* 119:164 "Seven times daily I praise Thee." The chapel became the focal point of the Brothers' lives.

First Chapel in De Soto

All of the Brothers were searching for a community prayer life to help develop a spirit of what it would mean to be a diocesan brother, especially a Diocesan Brother of Blessed Pius X. Most religious communities emulated the spirit of their founder and created prayer forms and styles which would help them live out that spirit. The Brothers had to find their own. Certainly the recitation of the Divine Office and the evening Holy Hour went a long way to help them in trying to follow the spirit of Blessed Pius X. That spirit, "to restore all things in Christ," was their aim and goal.

Bishop Treacy, Father Roemer and all the Brothers struggled with just what was the identity of a Diocesan Brother. Many people in the Church found it difficult to understand the role of the Brother to begin with. The vocation of a Brother is not well understood even today. Throughout the centuries, the Church had two distinct groups of Brothers. One group consisted solely of brothers. Other groups had priests and brothers, such as the Crosier Fathers and Brothers. Both groups, however, took the vows of poverty, chastity and obedience. Brothers, in many different ways, were auxiliaries to the priests, with many of them being known at the time as "hewers of stone and drawers of water." In other words, they usually engaged in manual labor to support the life of the community. However, the De La Salle Christian Brothers were an example of a community totally dedicated to education. In some groups, the Brothers were distinguished by the type of work they did.

A Brother was to be a man of God, a man who dedicated his life to Christ. It was a total commitment that was not to be taken lightly. A Brother strived to become more Christ-like and to bring peace and love, as well as the joy of Christ, to others. A Brother lived in community with his confreres who had made the same dedication; they lived, worked and prayed together. Brotherhood required sharing with one another, and attempting to help each other grow and deepen in faith and commitment to Christ.

In the Constitutions and Directives adopted at the General Chapter of the Brothers of St. Pius X in August of 1975, the Brother's Community had come to understand a Brother of St. Pius X as follows:

> Let us never forget the obligation we have of one another in the fellowship of our Community. Let us go out to one another freely in friendship and love. Let us pray for and with one another joyfully, sharing not just our material goods, but our spiritual gifts as well, that we may draw encouragement from our common faith and hope. Let us speak the truth to one another in the spirit of gentleness and humility, and be ready to acknowledge weakness, to accept and forgive each other as freely as God has accepted and forgiven us; to bear one another's burdens, fulfilling the law of Christ; to heal and support one another in love without thinking of ourselves.

This, for the time being, provided a glimpse of the vocation of a Brother.

Great tasks faced the Brothers. It seemed as if their life as a Brotherhood centered around three goals:

a) to develop a spiritual life as a Community and as individuals,

b) to grow in understanding what it meant to be a Brother, as well as a member of a Diocesan Brotherhood,

c) to do the necessary manual labor of providing a place to live and food for the table.

The monastery in De Soto

The good people of De Soto were stunned. Who was this group called the Brothers of Blessed Pius X? Those who were Catholic were somewhat familiar with Catholic religious institutions, but De Soto was predominately Protestant. Here were five young men and a handsome priest! Why did they choose De Soto? Moreover, these men wore black and green, a combination even Catholics had not seen before! One of the neighbor ladies thought that the Brothers were another "Boys Town." The Brothers did look rather wild. They hiked all over the bluffs, swam in the Mississippi, fished off the dock on Highway 35, played volleyball and did many other rugged things. But then, on warm summer evenings with the chapel windows open, people could hear the Brothers chanting the Divine Office, singing the Benediction Hymns and the Salve Regina. Slowly the people came to realize that the Brothers were there for a specific purpose: to live their religious commitment.

One of the first projects was to put running water into the house. About two-hundred feet from the main house was an artesian well. The standard saying was, "We had running water if we ran and got it." The Brothers began to dig a ditch six feet deep. In the process of digging, every time a train went by, part of the ditch would cave back in. Because the Brothers dug the ditch by hand, whenever it caved in, they had to throw the sand and dirt out again. Father Roemer's mother donated a pump. During this time showers were taken in a pond about a quarter of a mile away. Joe Malin, Richard Kimmet and Ed Penchi (later to become Father Ed Penchi), all from Genoa, helped the Brothers with the running water project. What a big help it was to have running water!

Digging the trenches for water pipes in De Soto; Brothers Thomas and Michael with neighbor Dennis Newton; Brother John looking on

The Brothers painted the exterior of all the buildings. It certainly helped to give everything a fresh look. The interior of the house needed renovation to help the house become livable. The Ghelfi's had not used the entire house, so some parts just needed a good cleaning. The three upstairs rooms were used by the four novices and the one candidate. Father Roemer's room, a crowded 10 x 12 foot area, was on the first floor. It was exceptionally small, and plans were made for an addition to the house to give him a larger living space consisting of a bedroom, bathroom and office. The dining room also needed to be enlarged. This was to be done within the next year.

New Friends and Neighbors

After the Brothers had been in De Soto for two days, two youngsters came to their door with a pan of freshly-baked rolls. "We are two of the Spalla kids; our mother baked these for you." Their parents, Herb and Rose, had sent the children to the Brothers' home. The people of De Soto, Rising Sun, Ferryville, Seneca, Genoa, Viroqua and the surrounding area were extremely generous to the Brothers. Beside the Spalla family, the following families were also of great help: Gillespie, Koch, Boardman, Hurm, Zielke, Maggio, Newton, Massie, Wolf, Walleser, Sallander, Sandvick, Prell, McDowell, Ghelfi, Scoville, Dyer, Garvey, Johnston, Finley, McNamara, Munson, Long, Seymour, Worman, Cole, Reagan, Stouvenal, Gordon, Gantenbein, Brown, Hickok, Becker, Mattson, Fox, Lucey, Arneson, Yaun and many others. The following Scriptural quote from the *Letter of St. Paul to the Thessalonians* (1:2-3) reflected the gratitude of the Brothers: "We always mention you in our prayers and thank God for you all, constantly remembering you before God our Father how you have shown your faith in action, worked for love, and persevered through hope, in our Lord Jesus Christ."

During the next few months, four fine young men became candidates: Don Bosco McDermott of Bernard, Iowa, Ralph Gianoli of Genoa, Wisconsin, Charles Bisenius of Cascade, Iowa and James Althoff of Earlville, Iowa. All four were between the ages of eighteen and twenty-two. Interestingly, the upheaval caused by the painting and renovating did not deter them from coming. They all pitched in immediately.

As word spread in De Soto and the surrounding area about the Brothers, warm and wholehearted acceptance was shown by people of all denominations, who became friends to the Brothers and offered their assistance whenever possible. Dennis and Mae Newton, an elderly Methodist couple, lived across the street. Often, the Brothers would ask to borrow Dennis's long ladder. One day Dennis came over to get his ladder to do a job at his own house. A new candidate had arrived and did not know that it was Dennis's ladder. When Dennis asked if he could use the ladder, the young candidate happily said, "Yes, Dennis, and any time you want to use it, you are welcome to it." Dennis got such a kick out of that remark that he went down to the lumberyard to tell Albert Munson. The story, of course, circulated throughout the town in a hurry. The Brothers possessed deep gratitude in their hearts for all of the people of De Soto and the surrounding area. Neighborliness ranked supreme among them.

First Rule

Each religious order and congregation has a Rule and Constitutions. Since the Brothers were in their first year of foundation, they had to write their own Rule and Constitutions. Bishop Treacy asked Father Edwin Thome, Assistant Chancellor at the time, to help Father Roemer draw up what they thought would be a suitable Rule and Constitutions. On the beautiful and warm sunny days of the summer of 1952, these priests would take a table outdoors, and under the shade of the maple trees on the front lawn, they formulated the Rule and Constitutions, which were used as the ideal and goal for the Community's first few years. The following paragraphs from the Rule are relevant:

4. No brother shall consider himself exempt from the general Rule of the house, but must look on it as a most efficacious means of sanctification.

5. He shall raise his heart to God often each day by prayer and renew his intention of doing all things for God's honor and the salvation of souls.

9d. Dressing should be rapidly but not slovenly.

25. Lights must be out by 10 p.m.

Later on in this brief history, parts of the New Rule and some of the Constitutions which were adopted in 1975 will be mentioned to contrast the old and the new Rule and Constitutions. Father Thome later shared with Brothers throughout the years the experience of writing the Rule. In typical Father Thome style, he said that it was an "awesome and fantastic experience."

29

Father Roemer teaching the Rule to (L to R) Brothers John, Edward, Michael, Don Bosco, Joseph, Anthony, Charles, Martin, Francis and Richard

The religious formation of candidates and novices had always been a major concern of all religious orders. Father Roemer inaugurated a definite program of studies in September of 1952:

> Spiritual Life: three times a week
>
> Old Testament: twice a week
>
> New Testament: twice a week
>
> Liturgy: once a week
>
> Gregorian Chant: twice a week
>
> Catechetics: twice a week

These studies, along with study and explanation of the Rule, laid the groundwork for the beginning of the Brothers' religious and spiritual formation. Moreover, with the prayer life of the Community and the thirty minutes allowed each day for spiritual reading, each novice and candidate thus had the opportunity to grow religiously in mind and heart. However, with all of the work to be done, it was almost impossible to maintain such a full schedule.

Dairy Cattle

In August, Father Roemer mentioned that it would be nice to have some cows so the Brothers could have their own milk and meat. It was at this time that candidate Wilfred (Michael) Mandernach asked his parents if they would be willing to donate some cows. They were pleased to give three, and all had been bred. Brother John's brother again volunteered his truck, and the cows arrived on August 15. Daisy, Lizzie and Betsy made the trip well. On August 30, Daisy gave birth to a little heifer calf that was named Judy.

The cattle had to be milked and fed, the rest of the building renovation required completion, wood had to be cut for the winter, fences needed to be repaired, and a thousand other projects had to be undertaken just to get ready for winter. The families of Brothers John and Thomas obtained many items for the Brothers and came often to help with organizing the kitchen and other projects. Since Ralph was from Genoa, the people of St. Charles Parish, as well as the parishioners from Rising Sun, Seneca and Viroqua, helped provide feed for the cattle. Sometimes there was so much to do that it seemed classes had to be neglected. Financially, the Brothers were totally on their own, and it was necessary that these things be done. Thus, the novitiate program could not always follow the plan that had been envisioned. The Brothers did what had to be done. The novitiate was still a good one, even though it did not always follow the pattern desired.

It was at this time that Mr. Richard P. Loftus, who had donated the property, came for a visit. He was amazed at the work that had been done and was extremely pleased. Unfortunately, during his trip, he and his mother were in a serious car accident just outside of Victory, Wisconsin. Mrs. Loftus was quite shaken up and taken to St. Francis Hospital in La Crosse. Fortunately, there were no broken bones and no serious injuries. Mr. Loftus had been given a relic of Blessed Pius X, and he attributed this fortunate escape to the intercession of the Brothers' patron.

First Christmas

Christmas was always a delightful time in a monastery. During the Advent season, the Brothers sang the "Rorate" while lighting the candles on the Advent wreath.

Drop down dew ye heavens from above

And let the clouds reign down the Just One . . . (Isaiah 45:8)

All of the Brothers sent out a lot of Christmas cards to their families and friends, as well as to those friends they had made within the Community. Brother Thomas and candidate Charles Bisenius, both good singers, directed the choir in preparation for Midnight Mass at Sacred Heart Church in De Soto. Father Roemer celebrated Midnight Mass with the parishioners and Brothers participating. The people of Sacred Heart Parish and the Brothers formed a unique bond of friendship throughout the years. There was a mutual support and admiration on both sides which remains today.

Father Roemer and the Brothers of Blessed Pius X wish you a joyous Christmas and pray that the peace of Christ may be with you throughout the year.

The Brothers' First Christmas Card, 1952

The Brothers' first Christmas was most rewarding. God's people contributed $880 in donations and food items. Father Roemer used to say that St. Joseph was the Brothers' procurator, with all the financial needs of the Community placed in his hands. Because St. Joseph was also a patron of the Brothers, they hoped that he would keep a special eye on them, and it seemed that he always came through.

New Candidates 1953

The year 1953 began with a new candidate. George Bellman of Bremerton, Washington arrived on January 2. The novitiate class consisted of Wilfred Mandernach, Don Bosco McDermott, Ralph Gianoli, Charles Bisenius and George Bellman. On June 12, 1953 these five candidates were invested as novices and took the following names:

Wilfred Mandernach	Brother Michael
Don Bosco McDermott	Brother Don Bosco
Ralph Gianoli	Brother Anthony
Charles Bisenius	Brother Charles
George Bellman	Brother Mark

THE PAX

In March of 1953, the first issue of THE PAX was published. It was a four-page pamphlet sent out to friends letting them know what was happening with the Brothers of Blessed Pius X. After many suggestions, all agreed that THE PAX would be the title. PAX was a prominent symbol for the Brothers, since it was part of the habit. Also, Blessed Pius X gave his life for the cause of peace. No one more than he, up to this time in history, had extended the sign of peace to the modern world. Because true peace could not come from any source other than Jesus, the Brothers wanted this bulletin, THE PAX, to be a sign of peace to their friends.

THE PAX was published monthly for nearly twenty-four years. The number printed went up to 24,000, and THE PAX was sent to every state, as well as to several countries. It kept the Brothers' families and friends informed about the development of the new Community. It also served as a means of advertising the various Field Masses and other events which the Brothers would have as time went on. Probably most beneficial of all, was that it gave readers an understanding of what a Brother's vocation was and why young men would want to pursue that type of consecrated life.

THE PAX contained much spiritual advice and recommendations, especially in the column of the Director. Each month, Fathers Albert

Roemer, George Passehl and Albert Raschke, and Brothers Kevin Brutcher, Conrad Henninger and Michael Mandernach wrote a column during their stint as Director. Most of the other articles in THE PAX were written by the Brothers themselves, though the authors' names were not given.

Each month's issue contained a column called "News of the Brothers." The events happening within the Community, and the ministries of the Brothers were shared. Many times, humorous interchanges between Brothers were also shared. One of the stories shared was the time candidates Anthony and Michael, who looked alike, possessing the same height, weight and hair color, went to pick up a load of hay from a friend near Viroqua. The old truck broke down; it took longer than expected. They missed lunch and subsequently were also late for dinner. Accordingly, they decided to stop for a bite to eat. As they sat down in the booth at the restaurant, the waitress came and said, "Oh, twins!" Without hesitation or blinking an eye, candidate Anthony said, "No, we're Brothers, but we don't have the same father and mother!" That really confused her. Through THE PAX, people were able to get a good idea of each Brother's personality.

"I got the trump card!"

Brothers (L to R) Anthony, Francis, Joseph Spasaro and Thomas

Many people requested prayers of the Brothers. Prayer intentions from the April 1953 edition of THE PAX were as follows: a happy marriage, return of relatives to the Faith, employment, men and women in the military, an Army pilot who was reported missing and recovery of health.

One of the chaplains at St. Rose Convent felt quite proud of the little publication and the PAX emblem. He was Father Victor Pax. We called him the "big Pax;" we were the "small Pax." THE PAX also included many humorous incidents known about Blessed Pius X. One time, the great Italian magician Fregoli, a master of illusion, had an audience with the Pope. After his performance, the Pope said to him, "If you can remain Fregoli for a moment, I'll bless you, and then you may change into anyone you like."

The last issue of THE PAX was published in December of 1977. It was the Christmas issue. The last page of that issue had the words PEACE ON EARTH written on it. This was unplanned, but very appropriate!

The Auxiliary

In the first issue of THE PAX, permission had been given by Bishop Treacy to begin the Auxiliary for the Brothers of Blessed Pius X. What was the Auxiliary? It was simply a group of people who helped the Brothers spiritually and financially. Individual yearly members contributed $2.00, family members $5.00 and perpetual members $25.00. In turn, all helpers of the Brothers shared in all of the daily prayers and works of the Brothers. The intentions of the Auxiliary members were included in daily Mass, recitation of the Divine Office and the nightly Holy Hour. Members of the Auxiliary were asked to join the Brothers in praying for world peace and reciting the *Prayer of Blessed Pius X* each day. It was recommended that they do all in their power, by prayer and example, to foster the spirit of Blessed Pius X through active participation in the liturgy, frequent Communion and promotion of the lay apostolate.

Father Roemer's mother formed a group of ladies in Wilmette, Illinois into an Auxiliary. They met each month for prayer and a card game. The proceeds were given to the Brothers. Other groups formed in De Soto, La Crosse, Port Edwards and other places. Many people responded by mail. These groups and individuals which made up the Auxiliaries were a source of great financial aid in the early days of the Brotherhood.

Bishop Treacy

THE PAX contained much about the life of Bishop John P. Treacy. He was born in Marlboro, Massachusetts on July 23, 1890. He attended Holy Cross College in Boston, Massachusetts, Catholic University in Washington D.C. and St. John's Seminary in Brighton, Massachusetts. He was ordained for the Diocese of Cleveland, Ohio on December 8, 1918. After serving as assistant pastor for twelve years in various Cleveland parishes, he was named Diocesan Director of the Society for the Propagation of the Faith, an office he held for fourteen years. He distinguished himself in this office by an ardent zeal for the Missions. He was also active in retreat work.

The Most Reverend Amleto Giovanni Cicognani, Apostolic Delegate to the United States, ordained Father Treacy a Bishop in St. John's Cathedral in Cleveland on the Feast of the Guardian Angels, October 2, 1945. He was appointed Coadjutor Bishop of La Crosse at that time; he was made Ordinary of the Diocese on July 23, 1946. Bishop Treacy loved pomp and pageantry, and everything he did had a certain flair. Every January 6, the anniversary of the foundation of the Brothers, he brought to De Soto the group of men known as the Ancient Order of Acolytes, who were Mass servers on certain occasions for the Bishop. All enjoyed a wonderful meal, after which they participated in the evening Holy Hour and adoration. Then Bishop Treacy entertained the Brothers and guests with stories and with his hopes and dreams for the Brothers. Each time the Bishop visited he played the piano, and all would sing. His presence always delighted the Brothers, as he took a personal interest in each one.

On the fifth anniversary of the foundation of the Brothers, the following was written in THE PAX:

After the evening devotions he spoke to the Brothers. He stated that he was much impressed with the chanting of the Divine Office. The manner of the Brothers' participation in this function indicated, he stated, that a spirit of true devotion was gradually being formed. The Brothers ought to feel happy about the fact that their prayers have been a factor in the development of a spirit of faith in the entire diocese. The Brothers...can share in the work of Catholic Action. Already in the short period of five years the Brothers have helped in the running of the Seminary. Now they are helping with the care of the children at St. Michael's Home. Some also have been and are engaged in the catechetical apostolate. What a truly splendid work this is! Bishop Treacy then emphasized the necessity of solid spiritual formation. "It is necessary," he said, "for the Brothers to acquire a spirit of perseverance in their vocation and to become solidly established in their calling. Special formation is most necessary for all. Once the Brothers are firmly established, active work will be found in abundance. Every talent can be used in the service of God. Of the many virtues necessary in religious life, total dedication through obedience stands out most prominently. An obedient man, even though he may lack talents, can accomplish great things for God. The Brothers should become ready through obedience to take up every work.

Whenever Bishop Treacy was asked what kinds of ministries the Brothers would do, he responded, "Their work will be as broad as the Church."

Bishop Treacy at the piano with the Brothers - L to R: Brothers Peter Thomas, Thomas, Cletus, Joseph, Stephen, Dominic, Alcuin, Aquinas and Edward

2   Growth

Catechetical Opportunities

In the spring of 1954, sometime in early April, Father Francis Phalen of St. Mary's Parish in McGregor, Iowa came with a special request: Would four of the Brothers teach catechism to the students of St. Mary's for two weeks beginning on May 16? One of the goals of the Brothers had always been to be involved in religious education. And now, here was the golden opportunity. Father Roemer, much to the delight of all the Brothers, assured Father Phelan that four Brothers would be happy to teach.

Brothers Charles, Thomas, Martin and Richard were selected. Brother Charles taught 7th and 8th graders, Brother Martin 5th and 6th, Brother Richard 3rd and 4th, and Brother Thomas taught the 1st and 2nd graders. They lived in the rectory with Father Phelan and taught after the 8:00 a.m. Mass from 9:00 a.m. until 3:00 p.m. The *Baltimore Cathechism, Jesus and I* charts, and other available catechetical materials of the time were used. The Brothers were now doing what many of them had envisioned doing when they joined the Community. They were fulfilling the spirit of Blessed Pius X, who was concerned about religious education for children as well as for adults. The Brothers were given the opportunity to make a difference in the lives of these students, and they took advantage of it, making the Faith both enriching and fun for students.

At recess, the Brothers played ball with the students. They ate with them at noontime, and shared all kinds of other activities. The 7th and 8th

grade boys of St. Mary's formed a baseball team and even played against St. John's of Prairie du Chien, Wisconsin. Brother Charles claimed that the boys from St. Mary's won the game. A May Crowning ceremony was arranged on the last evening of the Brothers' stay. One of the 8th grade students was chosen as the May Queen, and six others formed the Queen's court. Brothers Charles and Richard decorated the Marian altar, while Brothers Thomas and Martin taught Marian hymns. Every ounce of energy was put into the program, and the parents were delighted with the results. To them, the "Brothers in green" were an answer to prayer. All in all, this first experience of teaching religion opened a door to a great apostolate for the Brothers.

First catechetical assignment at St. Mary's, McGregor, Iowa

L to R: Brother Charles, Brother Richard, Father Francis Phelan, Brother Martin, Brother Thomas,

St. Pius X had said that ignorance of divine truths was responsible for the evils in the world. With determination, he began his catechetical reforms, urging the laity to do their part in the work of imparting truths of the Faith. Because divine life, which flows from the altar, is the source of all apostolic activity, Pius X permitted children to receive Holy Communion at the age of reason. He startled the world by doing so. He encouraged the laity to receive Communion daily. At this time, the Brothers were helping students to prepare for their First Holy Communion and were happy to share in this ministry.

The next fall, the Brothers began teaching at St. Wenceslaus in Eastman, Sacred Heart in Wauzeka, St. James in Rising Sun, St. Patrick's in Seneca, St. Philip's in Soldiers Grove, Sacred Heart in De Soto and St. Mary's in Gays Mills, all within the Diocese of La Crosse. Every Saturday, two cars of Brothers left from De Soto early in the morning to "teach as Jesus did." The pastors were delighted, and the Brothers were overjoyed.

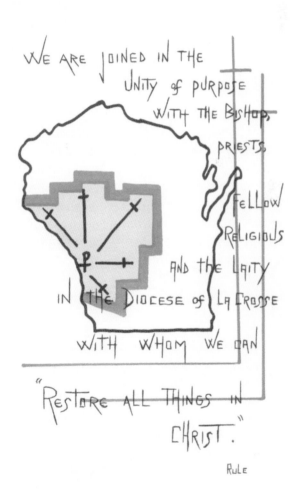

Map of the Diocese of La Crosse (drawn by Brother Gary Smith)

To prepare well, the Brothers were in need of training in Scripture, theology and teaching methods. Most of the Brothers were now teaching and attended instructional classes presented by Father Francis Wavra, the Diocesan Confraternity Director, and Sister Rose Rita Collignon, FSPA. Along with the classes that Father Roemer taught each morning, this training helped form the Brothers into good catechists.

The two-week Summer Vacation Religious Program became another part of the religious education of these parishes. Many had programs in place, but now the Brothers were given the opportunity to teach. Monsignor Urban Baer in Eastman, Father Francis Zoll in Seneca, Father Roman Kirin in Soldiers Grove, Father Henry Cassidy in Wauzeka, Father Francis Rushman in Gays Mills, and Father Chester Wrzaszczak in De Soto and Rising Sun, the pastors of these parishes, were supportive and open to the Brothers catechizing in their parishes. The summer program sometimes required the Brothers to live in the rectory with the pastor. In many instances, strong bonds of friendship developed between the pastor and the Brothers. The Brothers began to feel more a part of the diocesan catechetical ministry because of this.

Word circulated in the Archdiocese of Dubuque, Iowa that the Brothers had taught Summer Vacation Religious Education at St. Mary's in McGregor. Soon, Father Karl Klein of Volga and Wadena requested teachers for his summer program. Father Vincent Simon of Hanover, Father Robert Rahe of Wexford and Father Duane Raftis of Dorchester also requested teachers for their Monday evening sessions. The Brothers went to all of them with eagerness and delight. As new Brothers came, they were incorporated into the catechetical ministry.

The Community diary for May 17, 1957 states: "May saw the Brothers begin their catechetical teaching for the Summer Vacation School:

Volga, Iowa	Brothers Dominic and Peter Thomas
McGregor, Iowa	Brothers Charles, Stephen, Aquinas and Joseph
Rising Sun, Wisconsin	Brothers Anthony and William Robert
De Soto, Wisconsin	Brothers Michael and Thomas"

The Evangelical Counsels: Poverty, Chastity, Obedience

In the summer of 1953, after the completion of a year of novitiate, Brothers John, Thomas and Francis made a retreat at the Trappist Monastery near Dubuque in preparation for their profession of promises. In a private ceremony after their retreat, the three of them professed yearly promises of poverty, chastity and obedience.

Poverty, simply stated, meant that the Brothers shared their goods and gifts in common, lived a simple and dedicated life, and realized that, as individuals and as religious, they depended on God. To live chastely, they chose to love and serve God and all of God's people, rather than to love one person exclusively, as in marriage. They offered their celibacy as a witness and testimony of God's love. In obedience, they lived together as Brothers in Community and obeyed the will of God by taking part in the goals, hopes and works of the apostolate as envisioned by their Constitutions and as expressed through their superiors. It was not until August 21, 1973 that any of the Brothers made a permanent commitment to the Congregation. Up until that time, every Brother who had made yearly promises would renew those promises each year. This meant that every year, each one went through the process of discerning whether or not to renew. Most would renew, but once in a while, a Brother would not.

Second Investiture

The second investiture was held on June 12, 1953 at St. Joseph's Cathedral in La Crosse. The five postulants being invested were Brothers Charles Bisenius, Don Bosco McDermott, Anthony Gianoli, Mark Bellman and Michael Mandernach. Father Roemer told the congregation of over two-hundred people that the "worth of the Brothers was to be estimated by the spirit in which they give of themselves to God and to their Community. Their chanting of the Divine Praises in the Breviary, their daily Holy Hour, in which they offer reparation, will bring countless blessings." Brother Anthony had his troubles on investiture day. By mistake, he took one of Father Roemer's cassocks to be blessed instead of his own. As to length, it just fit; but in width, well, it was just a little too big. He wondered whether this would make him a candidate for "Director of the Brothers." Thus, the five began their year of novitiate, a year of intense spiritual formation and prayer.

Letter to the Apostolic Delegate

Just prior to the second investiture ceremony, Bishop Treacy wrote the following letter to the Apostolic Delegate to the United States, Archbishop Amleto G. Cicognani, D.D. in Washington, D.C. It was dated May 28, 1953:

Your Excellency:

In January 1952, we assembled four men under the direction of Father Albert P. Roemer, one of our most spiritual priests, an association to live a common life and to be known as the Brothers of Blessed Pius X. They began very humbly in one of the buildings which had been used as part of our temporary Seminary. God has blessed our adventure very generously, and now within less than two years after the establishment, they have been given a two hundred acre property thirty miles south of La Crosse and are raising cattle to help supply some of their food.

They have grown to the number of ten and are leading a fairly strict religious life, reciting in common each day the entire Divine Office in English in their temporary and beautiful chapel. This feature alone has proven quite attractive to the neighbors, and on Sundays their visitors are numerous to hear them recite Vespers and Compline and later in the evening Matins and Lauds. We have adopted part of the Franciscan and a few items of the Dominican Rules. I am enclosing for Your Excellency some literature which the Brothers have gotten out in the last year.

Feeling that the Brothers of Blessed Pius X are now on a secure foundation, what would Your Excellency suggest as my approach in Rome for some recognition by Holy Mother Church and this new group?

Along with the Seminary, the success of this new foundation and the enthusiasm with which our diocesan priests have accepted it have been the greatest possible comfort and encouragement to me. Any help or suggestions which Your Excellency can give me, as I prepare to leave for Rome, will be greatly appreciated.

With continued sentiments of gratitude to my dear consecrator, I am

Devotedly in our Lord,

John P. Treacy

Bishop of La Crosse

One can see that Bishop Treacy had great expectations for a positive response. Father Roemer and he waited anxiously for a reply from Rome. It came on October 29, 1953:

Most Reverend and Most Excellent Lord,

There has arrived at this Sacred Congregation for Religious the request from Your Excellency concerning the establishment of a new Congregation according to the norms of Canon 942, which will be called Brothers of Blessed Pius X.

Since the number of Brothers is quite small, this Sacred Congregation believes that the granting of this requested endeavor is to be disallowed until a more favorable time . . .

But when the number of Brothers has increased and with an approved common religious life, Your Excellency will again be able to recur to us, and, at the same time, provide other documents, namely:

1. to make known the first and last name of the founder and superior, both known as the Founder and also the first Superior, with a brief curriculum vitae (biography).

2. to make manifest the location for any extraordinary happenings, whether at the time of the establishment and as time goes on, such as visions and similar things, and those particular devotions and special acts of piety that must be brought forth (revealed).

3. to send a sample of the book of prayers, if such a special book is in use by the members.

I send you, Most Reverend Excellency, all good wishes and remain,

(Signed by the Secretary)

They had received their answer: wait and apply for formal recognition at a later date.

Canonization of Pius X

In the meantime, the whole Church was getting ready for the canonization of Blessed Pius X. The March 1954 issue of THE PAX announced this event:

On May 29, 1954, Blessed Pius X will be given the highest honors of the Church. He will be raised to the Altars and venerated as a saint. Hundreds of thousands are expected to be in Rome for the crowning event in the life of a humble peasant who rose to the sublime office of Vicar of Christ on earth. 'Let pilgrims flock together in great numbers and publicly and in the open give glorious expressions to their common faith,' said Pope Pius XII. His Excellency, Bishop Treacy plans to honor the occasion by celebrating a Pontifical High Mass on the outdoor altar of Holy Cross Seminary at 7:30 p.m.

A great crowd, nearly 1000 people, gathered for the Pontifical Mass. The Brothers were honored guests at the celebration. Father Roemer, the homilist, extolled the great virtues of St. Pius X. He said, "In every age God raises a saint who contradicts the spirit of that age. St. Pius X is a saint for the modern world. Imitation of his learning will destroy the false gods of modern pseudo-science. Imitation of his poverty will inspire us to put off the burdens of godless materialism and in all things seek first the Kingdom of God and His holiness. His pontificate is devoted to the restoration of all things in Christ through Mary." Then he gave a historical and inspiring account of the new Saint's life. He may well prove to be one of the most popular of all the saints.

Saint Pius X

The Community was now known as the "BROTHERS OF ST. PIUS X." They changed "Blessed" to "Saint" on the sign on the front lawn of their home on Old Highway 35 in De Soto.

Field Masses

Father Roemer was asked many times during his priesthood to be the Spiritual Director of pilgrims traveling to St. Joseph's Oratory, the largest shrine in the world in honor of St. Joseph, to the shrines of St. Anne de Beaupre and Our Lady of the Cape, all in Canada. He also accompanied various groups of pilgrims to Europe, for he was familiar with the spirit that existed at these places.

Whenever Father Roemer went on preaching assignments, a priest from the Seminary came to be with the Brothers at De Soto. Often Father McGarty would come. All the Brothers enjoyed his coming and friendships developed. He and other priests graced them with their presence and youthful enthusiasm for the Church.

Father Roemer's hope and dream was to have Field Masses for groups of pilgrims who would come to De Soto. The first Field Mass was planned for Sunday, August 16, 1954 on the Brothers' grounds in De Soto. It was to honor Mary during the Octave of the Assumption. The Feast of the Assumption had always been associated with Our Lady of the Harvest. The general intentions for the Mass were thanksgiving for the harvest and world peace. Harvest produce was brought to be blessed. All were encouraged to bring samples of their fruits, grains and vegetables as an act of thanksgiving. In the early Church, the faithful brought their gifts to the altar in solemn procession at the Offertory of the Mass. This gave all a sense of intimate participation. People were invited to do the same at this first Field Mass.

Field Mass in De Soto

48

The celebrant of the liturgy was Monsignor George A. Hammes, Chancellor of the Diocese of La Crosse. The homilist was Monsignor Thomas E. O'Shaughnessy. People came from the three-state area along with the Knights of Columbus, Legionnaires of Mary, Catholic War Veterans and Knights of St. Gregory. It was a wonderful celebration, the beginning of many more to come. Brothers Richard and Charles prepared the beautiful altar. The rest of the Brothers beautified the grounds and set up seating. Brother Thomas led the choir of Brothers and the congregation in singing.

Brothers Claude and Paul with pilgrims

The following year saw not only the Harvest Festival Mass on the Feast of the Assumption but also Masses in honor of St. Anne and St. Pius X. Busloads of people came from Minneapolis and St. Paul, under the leadership of Jane Martin, Marie Sarka and Ceil Tomas. Anatolia and Henrietta Dunn guided a group from Rochester, and Patrick O'Grady, a group from Chicago. For nearly fifteen years these groups, along with people from local areas, came to these outdoor Masses. After each Mass, a candlelight procession was held. The procession around the grounds and along the highway became a wonderful spectacle of faith. All of these groups, with ladies in their finery, processed down the slope of a small incline behind the Brothers' property on a simple dirt road. People loved it and would come back year after year.

The outdoor Masses were a means of advertising the Brotherhood as well as a means of support for the Brothers. They involved a lot of work, but they gave the Brothers another way to minister to people. That is what made them meaningful. The gatherings helped form friendships, many which last to this day.

Patrick O'Grady's pilgrims from Chicago

Candidates of 1954

From the summer of 1953 until the summer of 1954, more candidates arrived:

Francis J. Higgins	Winthrop, Iowa
Alfred Amorino	Oakland, California
John Debis	Staten Island, New York
Edward Zimmer	Spring Valley, Wisconsin
Richard Delaney	Peoria, Illinois
Otto Hommerding	Wausau, Wisconsin
George Cormier	Gardner, Massachusetts

Notice that the news of the Brotherhood had now spread throughout the whole country. About the time the Brothers of St. Pius X began, other Diocesan Brotherhoods also started. One, for example, was the Brothers of the Holy Rosary founded by Bishop Robert Dwyer in Reno, Nevada. The idea of Diocesan Brotherhoods was catching on.

The Brothers continued their religious life with prayer, spiritual reading and religious instruction, as well as their manual labor. In their classes, Father Roemer used the teachings of St. Thomas Aquinas, *Introduction to the Devout Life* by St. Francis de Sales and the Scriptures. This formation, along with Liturgy and Gregorian Chant, helped them to grow spiritually.

Manual labor consisted of taking care of cattle which, by that time, had increased to ten, cutting wood for the furnace and many repair jobs on the buildings. Stanchions and drinking cups for the cattle were put into the barn. Greg Lucey and Fred Smeby helped to cement the barn. The good people of Genoa, Seneca, Rising Sun, Viroqua and De Soto donated feed for the cattle. At least one of the candidates, John Debis, a native of New York, thought farming was hard work.

The buildings were beginning to look good. Over sixty gallons of white paint were put on the outside of the buildings and now, with running water inside and a decent room for Father Roemer, things were beginning to shape up. After the installation of an oil furnace, the Brothers had evenly-distributed heat. With the old wood furnace, it had been hard to control the temperature. Some days it would be so warm that the candles on the altar would melt; the next day, the holy water in the font would freeze. Thankfully, all of the Brothers were young and energetic!

On the Feast of the Sacred Heart, June 25, 1955, five young men were invested:

Richard Delaney	Brother Richard
Edward Zimmer	Brother Edward
Francis Higgins	Brother Martin
John Debis	Brother Francis
Otto Hommerding	Brother Joseph

Their small Community was growing. The Brothers who had finished novitiate that year and those from the year before, six in all, made promises in a private ceremony.

New Land

Greg Lucey and Father Roemer negotiated the purchase of the Nels Paulson farm five miles east of De Soto. There were a hundred acres of tillable land on the 120-acre-farm. Now the Brothers could produce the necessary feed for their cattle. Brother Anthony contoured the land, and with the help of Ed Scoville, purchased five young cows to help form a suitable herd of cattle. At last, the Community began to generate some income. The location of the farm was rather inconvenient because of the distance from where the livestock were housed, about five miles. All the feed had to be hauled down Lawrence Hill Road. It took much time either by tractor or truck, but the actual work time on the farm each day was rather short since all of the Brothers were expected to attend daily prayer services with the Community as well as classes. It did not leave much time for planting, cultivating and harvesting. But the Brothers were delighted to have the farm, because no longer did they have to rely on the good people of De Soto, Genoa and other areas for their feed.

This farming system was used until 1960, when the Brothers came to realize that the farming operation as it existed was not practical or feasible. Even though the land was excellent, and they had some good crops, too much time was spent running back and forth. Also, some of the equipment was old and a great deal of time was spent repairing it. Brother Anthony, kind and gentle man that he was, along with some of the other Brothers, became frustrated with the arrangement. Brother Thomas and he recommended to Father Roemer that different farming arrangements be pursued.

Colby

Father Roemer remembered preaching a Forty Hours Devotion at St. Mary's in Colby in the fall of 1952. At that time, Mr. and Mrs. George Steinwand had approached Father about wanting to give their farm to a religious community. They offered it to several different religious communities with no takers. After Father's initial visit in 1952, the Steinwands had written to him to ask the Brothers to pray for a religious community to come forth who wanted the land. One nice November day in 1959, Father Roemer and Brother Anthony took a trip to visit George Steinwand. (Mrs. Steinwand had died since Father Roemer's last visit). They wondered if George was still looking for a religious community to whom to give his farm. George was still willing to offer the farm. If the Brothers of St. Pius X wanted it, he would be delighted to give it.

"Home of Colby Cheese"

George contacted Mr. Frank Nikolay, an attorney from Abbotsford, to prepare the papers. The date was set to make the transfer of the property on December 31, 1959. On that day, Father Roemer and Brother Anthony traveled to Colby. They met Mr. Steinwand and Mr. Nikolay to complete negotiations and to sign the necessary papers. At that time, George mentioned that his wife, who had died in 1954, had had a great devotion to St. Pius X, and she, too, having been part of the original discussion about giving away the farm, would be most pleased.

Fr. Roemer with George Steinwand, the donor of the Colby property

In making the gift to the Brothers, George said, "I have received this farm from God, and my one desire is to give it back to God." The farm included two dwellings, one an eight-room house where Mr. Steinwand lived, another a five-room house in which his farm help had lived. It also included 100 acres of tillable land, twenty acres of virgin timber, a 100-foot barn, a machine shed and other small buildings. Father Roemer expressed his gratitude: "George made this donation in the name of the entire Steinwand family. George says he owes all that he has to his parents and members of his family, so he made this gift in their name and wanted them all to share in it."

Mr. Nikolay congratulated George on his gift, saying, "It would certainly help the cause of religion if more people were of the same frame of mind as Mr. Steinwand." Father John Pinion, pastor of St. Mary's in Colby, expressed satisfaction at the Brothers' coming to Colby and wished them every blessing in their new venture, offering his cooperation and assistance.

Colby farm

Plans were made to move the whole farming operation from De Soto to the Colby site. Brother Anthony was most delighted and made plans to move the cattle and machinery in the spring. Brother Thomas, a good remodeler, along with several of the postulants, began preparing the house to make it suitable for a novitiate. George, who moved to the smaller house, was delighted with the arrangements. He could continue to live there and was invited to have any of his meals with the Brothers. The Brothers were well-received in the Colby area. Whenever Brother Thomas or any of the Brothers were in need of some advice or conversation, the neighbors were always most kind. They even taught the Brothers how to play "Sheepshead," a card game most of the Brothers were not familiar with. The cattle and machinery were moved in spring.

In 1960, when the house in Colby was opened, a Harvest Mass was celebrated there. The heavy population of Catholics in that area made attendance at the Mass even greater. Three hayracks were set up to make an altar, which was surrounded with grain, corn, fruits and vegetables. With outdoor lighting and a large cross as the backdrop, it was a beautiful sight to behold. The event was well-advertised in Wausau, Eau Claire, Marshfield,

Neillsville and the surrounding areas. The August 1960 edition of THE PAX read:

> The first Field Mass at the Novitiate of the Brothers, one mile south and one mile west of Colby, will be held on Monday, the Feast of the Assumption, August 15, at 8:00 p.m. The site is the spacious farm formerly owned by George Steinwand. After the Gospel of the Mass the school children will carry samples of the harvest in procession while the Brothers and the congregation chant the harvest psalms of Thanksgiving. Father Albert Roemer will be the celebrant, assisted by Father Edward Penchi. Bishop Treacy will be in attendance.

Harvest Field Mass at Colby, Wisconsin

It was a wonderful celebration. The police estimated the crowd in attendance to be over 3,500 people. The candlelight procession after Mass was estimated to be about a mile in length. To accomplish all of this, Father

Roemer had assembled local people to help organize the event: George Steinwand, Andrew Kaiser, Nick Stuttgen, Rod Cook, Joe Feckhelm, Matt Allar, Arnold Ohlinger, Roland Brehm, Vince Foster, Lawrence Weber and Al Frane along with Brothers Thomas, Anthony, Alcuin and Matthew.

What a wonderful expression of faith in God! What a witness of thanksgiving for the wonderful gifts God had given the Brothers! The new house was located next to the Colby Cheese Factory, the same factory where Mr. Joseph Steinwand, a brother to George, had started processing Colby Cheese years before. To witness this many people celebrating Mass, praying the Rosary, singing Marian hymns and raising their candles during the singing of the Magnificat was a faith-enriching experience for all.

In the following years, an educational forum on agriculture was conducted as part of the celebration of the Field Masses. The forum helped farmers understand various political and social aspects of their occupations. The Brothers hoped that the forums would help farmers feel proud of their accomplishments in producing food to feed people and to inspire pride in being farmers.

The Field Masses in De Soto and Colby were a wonderful ministry for the Brothers. Along with the publication of 24,000 copies of THE PAX, the Field Masses helped put the Brothers, De Soto and Colby on the map. The wonderful people of De Soto and Colby, even those of different faiths, accepted the Brothers so well. All watched with a spirit of reverence and prayerfulness as they sensed what the Brothers were all about: to be witnesses of the presence of God in the life of every person. The Brothers of St. Pius X were Brothers to all.

Our Blessed Lady of the Fields

Holy Cross Seminary

The fall of 1954 marked another beginning. Bishop Treacy asked Father Roemer if five Brothers could be assigned to Holy Cross Seminary. Father Roemer was reluctant to split the group because, if five went to the Seminary, only six would remain at De Soto, along with a couple of candidates. He was unsure if the Brothers were ready to take on such an assignment and very concerned about the stability of the Community. Originally, Bishop Treacy had told Father Roemer that it would take at least five years before any such mission could be initiated.

Despite his initial reservations, Father Roemer made the announcement on September 11 that five Brothers would be assigned to Holy Cross Seminary in La Crosse. They were to attend Vocational School in the morning and work at the Seminary in the afternoon. All of the Brothers went to the Vocational School to take an aptitude test. Courses were available in carpentry, auto mechanics, body and fender work, shop and printing. A complete series of courses in clerical work were also available.

The historic date for the beginning of this mission was September 29, the Feast of St. Michael the Archangel. Those selected were Brothers John Resch, Don Bosco McDermott, Edward Zimmer, Martin Higgins and Michael Mandernach, who was named superior of the group. They were welcomed by Father Alfred Hebert, the Rector of the Seminary. Father James Coke was named their spiritual director. Brother John was trained as a boiler room attendant, Brother Edward in carpentry, Brother Don Bosco in shop, and Brothers Martin and Michael in the clerical field.

The Brothers were to live in the section of the Seminary which had been designed for the Sisters who had cooked there for a period of time. Each Brother had a private room, something they were not used to. A beautiful chapel was on one end of the hallway, and a recreation room overlooking the Mississippi on the other. They also had their own dining room.

Working at the Seminary afforded the Brothers many privileges and opportunities. One of those was attending the Dedication Ceremony of Christ the King Chapel. Samuel Cardinal Stritch, Archbishop of Chicago, honored the celebration with his presence. The Brothers had the occasion to meet personally with him. At the same celebration, Bishop Treacy introduced them to Archbishop Albert Meyer, Archbishop of Milwaukee, as well as to several other Bishops. It showed the Brothers a vision of the broader Church.

Working at the Seminary: Brother Martin (above); Brother John (below)

Once in a while, priests on the faculty would challenge the Brothers to a game of volleyball after the evening Holy Hour. Fathers Bernard McGarty (whose parents were good friends of the Loftus'), Gerald Fisher, George Hinger, Andy Karobilis and others would show the Brothers how to play "real volleyball." This, along with their other associations, helped develop bonds of friendship and partnership. Not only were the Brothers privileged to work alongside these priests, but they could all have fun together.

Developing A Unique Diocesan Charism

Two questions in the minds of the Brothers were always "What is a Brother and who are the Brothers of St. Pius X?" Since many people asked them the same questions, most of the Brothers themselves were searching for the answers. Many of them had preconceived notions of "Brothers," but struggled to find meaning in their lives. What did it mean to be a religious in the Church? Who were "Brothers"?

The history of lay brothers, or religious brothers as they were sometimes called, dated back to the early Church. Brothers were found in the earliest monasteries. In fact, many monasteries themselves were founded by men who were not priests, but who dedicated their lives to God under the strict interpretations of the Evangelical Counsels of poverty, chastity and obedience. Two Brothers who founded monasteries were St. Anthony, in the Theban Desert and St. Francis of Assisi. There were other notable monastic figures who were Brothers, not priests.

The Brothers knew that prayer was a vital part of their dedication and life to God. Prayer was essential. Prayer was communication with God. The Brothers began each day with the celebration of Mass, the "source and summit" of their life. In chanting the Divine Office, they participated, with the Universal Church, in prayer. The Brothers' daily Holy Hour manifested their belief in the presence of Jesus in the Eucharist. The closing of each day's prayer with the singing of the "Salve Regina" manifested their dedication to Jesus through Mary.

> Salve Regina, mater misericordiae;
> vita, dulcedo et spes nostra, salve.
> Ad te clamamus, exsules filii Hevae.
> Ad te suspiramus, gementes et flentes
> in hac lacrimarum valle.
> Eia ergo, advocata nostra,
> illos tuos misericordes oculos
> ad nos converte. Et Jesum,
> benedictum fructum ventris tui,
> nobis post hoc exsilium ostende.
> O clemens, O pia, O dulcis Virgo Maria.

The Brothers knew the difference between a brother and a priest. Even though they were often called "Father," they knew that they were not ordained. Since most of the ministries in the apostolate would be carried out in association with diocesan priests, they came to learn that diocesan priests did not profess the Evangelical Counsels as do priests and brothers in religious orders and congregations. Moreover, the Brothers understood that each religious order or congregation has its own special charism, and that each religious congregation strived to fulfill a mission in the Church through community. This Community could be contemplative or engaged in apostolic activity.

The canonization of St. Pius X did much to help the Brothers in developing a unique charism as a religious diocesan institute. As St. Pius X's virtues became known to the world, the Brothers also began to have a distinct sense of what it meant to put into practice the ideals of humility and dedication that had been lived by their patron. St. Pius X was called the "children's Pope." His special interest was the spiritual welfare of children. "Holy Communion is the shortest and surest way to heaven," he wrote to all Catholics in 1906, urging frequent, even daily Communion, if possible. On August 8, 1906, he directed that children be permitted to receive their First Holy Communion as soon as they were able to understand the difference between the Sacred Species and ordinary bread. Holy Communion, he pointed out, was not a reward for virtue. It was a spiritual medicine to help people to resist temptation. It was this spirit which helped the Brothers in their ministry of catechetics. They were now doing what St. Pius X had emphasized as Pope. Children became a focus in their ministry.

Soon after the canonization of St. Pius X, Father Anselmo Onori, the Assistant Postulator of the Cause for the cause of Sainthood for St. Pius X, heard about the Brothers of St. Pius X in the Diocese of La Crosse. He visited them for a few days, participating in all of their spiritual exercises. It was a delightful time. After he left, the Brothers requested some item of St. Pius X that would remind them

Father Anselmo Onori with Brother Francis (L) and Brother Michael (R)

of him. "Sure," he said. "I have the perfect gift for you." It was one of the Pope's skull caps, known as the "zucchetto." It had been proudly displayed in the Brothers' monastery all these years.

St. Pius X's simplicity of life and humility of spirit helped the Brothers understand the need to live the simple life of poverty. His last will and testament said, "I was born poor, I have lived poor, and I wish to die poor." How well he demonstrated this throughout his life. This spirit of poverty was manifested in the Brothers' Rule: WHAT LOVE REQUIRES. This rule stated, "Poverty is a response to the call to respect God's creation. In trusting in the providence of God our Father, we follow Christ, and desire to imitate Him in the use of this world's goods. Being a disciple of Christ, poverty calls for a conversion of our minds, heart, and attitudes. It is necessary in our daily lives to witness to authentic poverty, which is the limited use of goods as required by our duties. An essential aspect of poverty is to bear witness to the human meaning of work which is carried out in liberty of spirit and restored to its true nature as the source of sustenance and service."

As the Brothers pondered the simplicity and life of St. Pius X, the idea of them receiving a monthly allowance was discussed. The decision was made to give each Brother ten dollars a month for personal expenses. Their diary stated that, "if a Brother receives money from home, he will apply it toward his allowance." Simplicity in practice and in heart was definitely part of the goal for the Community.

It was also on the occasion of the diocesan celebration of the canonization of St. Pius X that Bishop Treacy announced that a new parish would be established in La Crosse under the patronage of St. Pius X. It would be located on the south side of La Crosse. It was at this same parish that several of the Brothers ministered some fifteen years later, as CCD teachers, Director of Religious Education and teachers in St. Pius X Catholic School.

Sister Claretta, a Franciscan Sister of Perpetual Adoration in La Crosse, had painted a beautiful Coat of Arms of St. Pius X, containing the words "Instaurare Omnia in Christo," meaning "to restore all things in Christ." This magnificent wall painting graced the Brothers' home for sixty years, and St. Pius X's words became the Brothers' motto. They served as a reminder to the Brothers of their purpose as a religious Congregation and a reminder to each individual Brother to make the restoration of all things in Christ the focal point of his life and ministry. The Rule emphatically stated:

We are joined in the unity of purpose with our Bishop, priests, religious and laity in the Diocese of La Crosse with whom we can "restore all things in Christ." The Brothers of St. Pius X are a diocesan congregation that witnesses and serves the people of God in this Diocese. We, therefore, in response to the call of our Bishop, take upon ourselves the service of the Christian community, following the goals and needs of this Diocese.

The St. Pius X Coat of Arms

Pope of Peace

St. Pius X was known as the "Pope of Peace." In his book, "The Burning Flame," Francis Thornton wonderfully shared the passionate desire of St. Pius X for peace. In 1913, St. Pius X suffered an attack of what seemed to be influenza and was bedridden for twenty-one days. It left him rather weak. Being a man who loved hard work, he did not hesitate to go back to work immediately after recovery. But his radiance and smile seemed to be gone.

It was not the aftermath of the sickness that oppressed the Pope. In his mind and heart, he had the growing conviction that the world was moving toward a terrible tragedy. Often he shared his thoughts with Cardinal Merry del Val. St. Pius X talked about the terrible events which would soon happen. Merry del Val would probe the Pope for reasons for his concern, but St. Pius X would only say, "The great war is approaching." When Merry del Val argued that war did not seem to be imminent, the Pope responded with unusual gravity, "Your Eminence, things are going badly; we shall not get beyond the year 1914."

St. Pius X sensed what was in store for the world. He toiled from the first morning light until far into the night. He wanted to restore all people to love and serve Christ. But all he did seemed to be of no avail. Secret agreements, alliances, plots and counter plots were being enacted. The great navies of the world and increasing armies were forming. "Peace!" the Pope cried. The condition for peace, he insisted, was love. St. Pius X thought he had failed. He hated bloodshed; the very sight of blood sickened him. In 1914, the world would be overwhelmed with evil and death. The Pope's prophesy of the exact year came true with a suddenness that surprised everyone except St. Pius X.

The ambassador of Austria, along with a group of bemedaled assistants, petitioned him: "Holy Father, thousands of Catholics will march in the armies of Austria and Germany. Will you bless our armies in the struggle?" St. Pius X grasped the arms of his throne, his knuckles shone white, and a bright spot of red flamed up in his cheeks. "I bless peace, not war," he said. Thereafter, he told the Bishops, "Every avenue of peace must be explored. Priests and people must pray. There is no worthwhile victory in the world but the victory of peace." Many times, he would say, "I would be happy to give my own life if this chalice might pass from the world."

PAX symbol

PAX, (peace) became the symbol of the Brothers of St. Pius X. Their scapulars bore the PAX emblem. At the time when the Brothers of St. Pius X made permanent commitments, each Brother was given a ring on which PAX was engraved. The Rule quoted the *Letter of St. Paul to the Colossians* (3:15): "Christ's peace must reign in your hearts, since as members of one body, you have been called to that peace." This spirit of peace, so profound in the life of St. Pius X, was instilled in the heart and mind of each Brother.

Candidates of 1955

There were five candidates in 1955:

William Callari	Escanaba, Michigan
James Riley	Ashland, Wisconsin
John Benware	Holland, Michigan
James Donnan	Dubuque, Iowa
Donald Scott	Columbus, Ohio

Space Required

Living peacefully in a religious Community was a goal that at times could be difficult to achieve. The living facilities for the Brothers were such that at least two Brothers roomed together, sometimes as many as four. The rooms were not very large. In a space of 12 x 16 feet, there could be four Brothers. Bunk beds were used. Each Brother had a desk and they usually shared a common closet. It was crowded. In order to deal with some of the frustrations and tensions that arose, Father Roemer decided to have a weekly session to talk about the spirit in the house. This helped to "clear the air" regarding difficulties. Most of the time these sessions released the tensions.

The crowded conditions warranted building an addition to the main house in De Soto. Father Roemer needed more space, so an office-bedroom combination was constructed for him. An extension was added to the dining room. Even the small chapel in the main house had become inadequate, and a discussion began about the possibility of erecting a separate chapel. The Brothers felt they could do most of the work.

On June 17, 1955 the investiture ceremony included: William Callari (Brother Stephen), James Riley (Brother Ignatius) and John Benware (Brother Paul). At the investiture ceremony, it was announced that a new chapel would be built. Brother John Resch was transferred back to De Soto after one year at the Seminary; Brother Charles Bisenius was sent to replace him. Brother John became the general manager for the construction of the new chapel. The other Brothers and candidates were to help as much as they could, keeping in mind that catechetical assignments, the various Field Masses and other activities still had to go on. The chapel was to be 20 feet wide and 40 feet long. It would include a full basement, which would become the recreation room.

L to R: Brothers Michael, Leslie, Ignatius and John constructing the roof of St. Anne's Chapel

First, several small buildings had to be removed. The chicken coop and the outdoor "john" were torn down. There was just enough slope on the site for an outside basement door on the southwest corner, as well as two doors to enter the chapel. The basement was dug, and the pouring of cement for the foundation and the laying of blocks began. It was an exciting time. One could not help but think of the first verse of *Psalm* 84: "How lovely is your dwelling place, O Lord, our God." The objective was to make this chapel a special place. It was to be "done with the work of our own hands," an earthly

work in which the Brothers would celebrate the Sacred Liturgy of the Eucharist, chant the Divine Office, and have their daily Holy Hour.

Shortly after the construction of the chapel began, the Brothers had their annual retreat. Father Frank O'Hara gave the retreat. On July 21, 1955 just before dinner, he gave them a conference on death. Then the Brothers went to dinner. About two hours after dinner, eight of the Brothers and Father Roemer became sick and were rushed to St. Francis Hospital in

Brother Adrian rings the call to worship bell

La Crosse. It was what all suspected: ptomaine poisoning. It had been a very hot day. Mayonnaise, which was used to make a sandwich spread, was evidently the culprit. The Brothers and Father were released the next day. What a way to meditate on "death!"

Interior of St. Anne's Chapel

The interior of the chapel was knotty pine, with a cork-tone floor of various shades and a light green ceiling with transverse beams. The altar was made of oak with a green draped backdrop and a hand-carved crucifix. The PAX emblem was carved on the front of the altar. The exterior of the chapel, facing the highway, featured a niche for a statue of St. Pius X. Windowphanie, a paper material which looked like stained glass, was placed on the inside of each of the eight windows.

A few years earlier, a man from Cologne, Germany by the name of Frank Salzman, had heard of the Brothers and was interested in joining. He was about 60 years old. Father Roemer wrote to tell him that all of the Brothers were rather young and he might feel out of place. He recommended that Mr. Salzman join an order with older members. Mr. Salzman wrote back to say he understood and mentioned that he would send a gift. Four months later, a package containing a magnificent hand-carved wood statue of the Blessed Mother arrived. It was four feet high with exquisite features of Mary. The statue was placed on the left side of the altar with a spotlight over it. Each evening at the close of the Holy Hour, the spotlight was on Mary, and all other lights were turned off while the Brothers sang the "Salve Regina." A matching statue of St. Joseph was carved for the right side of the altar.

Wood-carved statue of the Blessed Mother

The goal to have the chapel completed by Christmas Eve was met. It was totally completed. The diary for December 24 read: "Gifts were opened at 9:00 p.m., after which Father Roemer took the Blessed Sacrament, and all the Brothers walked with him to the new St. Anne's Chapel. Many of the Brothers thought of the walk of Mary and Joseph with the unborn Infant to be born at Bethlehem that night. We chanted Matins in the Chapel and had Holy Hour. At 11:30, we went to Sacred Heart Church just a block away to sing Christmas Carols. Father Roemer celebrated the Midnight Mass. The third Mass on Christmas day was celebrated in our chapel. What a wonderful day to have our first Mass in our chapel. During the Eucharistic Prayer, Jesus became present on our altar, a gift of Bishop Treacy. We are deeply grateful to God for this little chapel. We are grateful to Father Roemer whose confidence and trust in God made it possible. And we are grateful to all the people who helped with this project."

The blessing of the chapel was set for January 8, 1956. Bishop Treacy blessed the chapel during a Mass celebrated by Father Roemer. Monsignor Anthony Wagener gave the homily to the 120 guests who were present. In his homily, Monsignor Wagener reflected: "A chapel gives permanency to an institution as the Blessed Sacrament is the center of Community life...in religious life members are taught self-denial, patience, and discipline, which lead to inner joy and peace." An open house was held all afternoon. A Holy Hour was celebrated at 3:00 p.m. The chapel, once again, was filled.

The diary for the day concluded as follows: "Today is a special day of rejoicing for the Brothers as God has blessed us so abundantly. We number 13 members: 11 Brothers and two postulants. We thank God for the many blessings He has bestowed on the Brotherhood. We thank Bishop Treacy for his words of encouragement, for his faith and trust in us and for all his acts of kindnesses. We thank Father Roemer on this day for his leadership, guidance and his ever- present encouragement to all the Brothers. Words will never be adequate to express all Father Roemer has done for the Brothers of St. Pius X. The new chapel is dedicated under the patronage of St. Anne. [This name was chosen in honor of Anne Loftus, who, with her son, generously donated the De Soto property to the Brothers.] We ask her to protect Jesus in the tabernacle as long as He will be there. We implore her to make this chapel a place of pilgrimage, something we have been praying for almost every day."

St. Michael's Home for Children

The second permanent mission in the Brothers' apostolate was St. Michael's Home in La Crosse, Wisconsin, where Brother Charles was assigned to work with the boys. A year later, Brothers Thomas and Don Bosco joined him. Brother Charles worked with the older boys, Brother Don Bosco with the middle group, and Brother Thomas with the smaller ones. It was a ministry they loved. Since the Brothers drove cars at that time, they would take the boys and girls to various events. Of course, that made them quite popular with the students. They were responsible for the boys from the time they finished school each day until the next morning when they went back to school. Unfortunately, the Brothers' time at St. Michael's Home spanned less than three years. The Brothers returned to De Soto, where many jobs awaited them.

Brother Thomas at St. Michael's Home for Children

Brothers Dominic, Charles, William Robert, Peter Thomas skating with boys from St. Michael's Home for Children

Adaptability

Monsignor James Finucan, secretary to Bishop Treacy, directed a day of recollection that fall. He maintained that the main virtue of a "Brother of St. Pius X" should be "adaptability." How prophetic his voice would be! After that presentation, Father Roemer had the Brothers rotate jobs such as cooking, cleaning, gardening, milking, etc., to become familiar with all aspects of Community living and Community responsibility. Especially was this to be done in the cooking area. It made for a variety of food. The meals made by Brothers with Spanish descent were quite a bit spicier than others. Every once in a while, there was also an exchange of rooms so that each Brother got to live with someone else. Yes, adaptability and flexibility were great virtues for a Brother to have.

With every good thing that was happening, there were also some things which were difficult. Brothers Martin Higgins and Richard Delaney left the Community in the fall. Both were such wonderful men, as were Brothers

Francis Peters and William Kundert. Even though new candidates came, these men had had a powerful influence among the Brothers. All went on to have great careers, and Richard Delaney became a priest in the Monterey, California Diocese.

As of September, 1955 the Community consisted of the following:

Brother John Resch

Brother Thomas McAllister

Brother Michael Mandernach

Brother Anthony Gianoli

Brother Don Bosco McDermott

Brother Charles Bisenius

Brother Edward Zimmer

Brother Francis Debis

Brother Otto Hommerding

Brother Stephen Callari

Brother Ignatius Riley

James Donnan, Postulant

Donald Scott, Postulant

Father Roemer appointed Brother Michael Mandernach to return to De Soto to be Brother Assistant and in charge of the office. Brother Francis was assigned to be Father John Paul's secretary and operate the switchboard at Holy Cross Seminary. Brother Thomas was appointed to replace Brother Martin at the Seminary.

Candidates of 1956

In 1956 a large group of candidates came:

John Nelson	Rochester, Minnesota
Melvin Welbes	Wausau, Wisconsin
Casimir Drzewiecki	Toledo, Ohio
James Lynch	Wichita, Kansas
William Ryan	New York, New York
Joseph Green	St. Louis, Missouri
James Henry	Norwood, Massachusetts

Assistant Directors

The steady influx of candidates prompted Bishop Treacy to appoint Father George Stashek, who had taught in high school and coached athletics, as Assistant Director to the Brothers. He had been a hospital chaplain and an assistant in parishes. Father's spiritual, mechanical, agricultural and physical talents were to be a great asset to the Brothers. "I am happy to be with the Brothers," said Father Stashek, "and I will do all I can to be of help."

Fr. George Stashek

Father Stashek was a great help as he assumed the responsibility of directing the work program of the Brothers, along with the teaching of classes. When Father Roemer was on preaching assignments, Father Stashek assumed the sacramental and liturgical responsibilities as well. Like Father Roemer, he was a man of great stature. No Brother would mess with him!!!

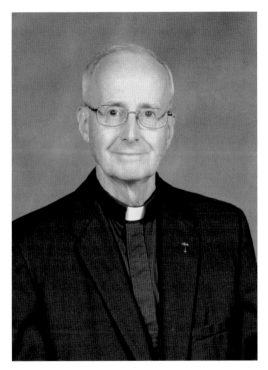

Father Edward Penchi

Father George Stashek had been the Assistant Director for one year when Father Edward Penchi was appointed to replace him. Father Penchi was well known to the Brothers, as he had helped to install the plumbing fixtures, etc. when the Brothers first arrived in De Soto. This was before he was ordained. He grew up in Genoa and knew the De Soto area well. Father Penchi was a cousin to Brother Anthony, who was elated when Father was appointed Assistant Director. At Father Penchi's ordination, Brother Anthony had carried Father's suitcase to his car and predicted, "Someday you might be appointed to the Brothers."

Father Penchi's role was that of Novice Master. He oversaw the spiritual formation of the novices and taught Catechetics, Liturgy and Gregorian Chant. He also took over the work program. Father's humble spirit and quiet presence affected all. His spirituality permeated the small religious house with a sense of peace and gentleness. Father Penchi's singing skills also enhanced the liturgical celebrations as he taught the beauty of Gregorian Chant, which St. Pius X had encouraged during his Pontificate.

Candidates of 1957

Constant concerns were having ample living quarters, stable financial means and proper spiritual formation for the Brothers. The next year saw the following candidates:

John Alvin	Richland Center, Wisconsin
Milo Duellman	Fountain City, Wisconsin
Jerome Krieg	Mosinee, Wisconsin
John Beckfelt	Grand Rapids, Minnesota
Richard Jira	Sioux Falls, South Dakota
Bernard Wavrunek	Neillsville, Wisconsin

Another outstanding group of young men with many different talents! All but Jerome were invested on October 17, 1957. Their respective religious names were:

John Alvin	Brother Jude
Milo Duellman	Brother Cletus
John Beckfelt	Brother Alcuin
Richard Jira	Brother Augustine
Bernard Wavrunek	Brother Bernard

With another five candidates, conversations began focusing on the possibility of adding living quarters as well as beginning a print shop. Both soon became a reality. Living space was definitely needed, and a print shop would provide a source of income. A two-story building to consist of eight rooms on the second floor and a dining room and kitchen on the first was planned. Again the Brothers did most of the work. This helped tremendously to alleviate the problem of cramped living space.

The Print Shop

Brother Adrian working in the Print Shop

The Print Shop began with the purchase of a 10 x 14-inch offset AB Dick printing press. THE PAX, letterheads, stationery, Christmas cards, and numerous other items were printed. Brother Dominic became one of the first operators. The printed word was one of the ministries of many monastic and religious communities. Through the operation of these presses, the teachings of the Catholic Faith reached multitudes of people. The Brothers hoped that they, too, could share in this apostolate in a small way. Their second hope was that it would generate income to help with the finances.

The Brothers' little printing press was running at fast speed most of the time. Orders of all kinds were coming in. Father Roemer had often talked about the possibility of publishing an area newspaper distributed to every household. It would be supported by ads and would include both religious and secular news, as well as local events. Brothers Dominic, Adrian and Paul were more than busy already. Brother Martin was busy with a variety of design work. THE PAX mailing list kept one Brother busy. Father Roemer thought that they could handle another newspaper. It was planned to print the first copy in January 1961. It was to be published monthly. Brother Charles was to get ads from local businesses in Viroqua, De Soto and Prairie Du Chien.

It was decided to call the paper THE VOICE OF PEACE. The first issue included a picture and story of ninety-seven-year-old Fred Bean, who still lived on a century-old farm six miles east of De Soto. Near the entrance of his house, two famous Indian trails crossed, the trail of the Blackhawk retreat and the Winnebago trail, which ran from Winneshiek Village (now De Soto) to a Winnebago town above the fork of the Kickapoo River at Manning. Fred was the youngest son of Doctor David Bean, the first physician of the Retreat, Wisconsin area.

Other articles in the paper featured such topics as the famous De Soto Historical Museum, where the paintings of C. M. Powell were entrusted to the care of Mr. Charles McDowell, a friend of Mr. Powell. The paper featured Mr. Frank Garvey of the Ferryville Bank, who had celebrated his fiftieth year in banking. One issue pictured Dennis Newton standing in the one-hundred-year-old cemetery at Rush Creek. The March 1961 issue included the story of the colorful week-long De Soto celebration at Bradenton, Florida commemorating the spot claimed by the great Spanish explorer, Hernando De Soto nearly 425 years ago, claiming those shores for Charles V and Spain.

Mrs. Thyra Hickok with antique German Bible

THE VOICE OF PEACE made the Brothers well-known in the area. For example, they were invited to attend such events as the dedication of the Little Brown School House in Redmond, Wisconsin. The School Museum was largely the work of Mabel Brasda. Pastor Anton Stury, a good friend of Father Roemer, gave the address at the dedication, and the De Soto High School Band provided the entertainment. The Brothers also watched the Old Timers' baseball game between the De Soto Black Sox, managed by Pat "Fred Haney" Gillespie, and the Ferryville Mudcats, managed by Bob "Casey" Dyer. This historic game was delightfully written up in the September issue of THE VOICE OF PEACE.

The March 1962 issue had a lovely picture of President John F. Kennedy with one of his famous quotes: "With a good conscience our only sure reward, with history the final judge of our deeds, let us go forth to lead the land we love, asking His blessings and His help, but knowing that here on earth God's work must truly be our own."

THE VOICE OF PEACE was only printed for two years. There were many reasons for its short duration. It became a financial burden, and it was difficult to get ads. In addition, the printing facilities were not adequate to print nearly 24,000 issues of THE PAX and 8,000 issues of THE VOICE OF PEACE. But it was a worthwhile endeavor while it lasted.

Barney

The story of Barney, the Brothers' pet dog, written by Father Roemer, appeared in both THE PAX and THE VOICE OF PEACE.

First of all Barney is very humble. He knows his place pretty well. He never comes into the house but is very content to remain in the barn. When as a young pup we took him along on walks, he would be afraid to walk over the rails that spanned a bridge. Then he would whine pitifully and wanted to be carried. If the bark of another dog was heard, Barney would come close to our heels.

As he was growing more mature, he became a little bolder in exploring the outside world. But if he strayed off the grounds just one sharp word, "Barney!" could cause his ears to drop. Then with his head dropped in humiliation and his flag lower at half mast, he would scamper to his place in the barn.

Barney

Routine life on monastic grounds gets a little monotonous for Barney. But like the good monk, he has a sense of humor that shows itself in little mischievous things that he does. When Brothers put their rubbers on the porch, Barney might drag one of them off and rustle it about. He knows it's wrong because, when he is reproved for it, he either rolls himself on the ground begging pardon, or else he comes slowly and meekly in a truly penitential spirit seeking a pat on his head as a token of renewed good will.

He plays amiably with the cats; but when the cats get serious about things, Barney has to give way. He is almost meek to a fault about his relations with other dogs of the neighborhood. One dog took a real "round" out of Barney. Barney put up little resistance and came away blood-stained. But the marvelous thing is that Barney holds no ill will nor does it dampen his spirits any. He always comes back for more and smiling.

One of the most remarkable virtues about Barney is his charity. He knows the routine of the Brothers. When they leave the house to go to the chapel, Barney parks himself right near the entrance. Here he awaits a pat on the head and makes a tenfold return of the charity by wagging his tail and showing great delight all over his being. In fact, sometimes it looks like his tail wags Barney.

If one brother shows him a little more affection, Barney will delay a little longer and give a few extra wags of his tail. But then, lest he slight anyone, he scampers off so that each receives some of his gladness.

Lately, he has taken on an authoritative role. When one of our neighbors came to our chapel for Mass, Barney sat squarely in front of the door and barked loudly. Not very apostolic of him! But then Barney apparently believes that monasteries are for monks and that it is better to keep the world out. We'll have to teach him differently. But in case he does this to any other visitors, all that they have to do is to say one loud word to Barney, and he will head off for the barn where things are more secure for him.

But if Barney thinks that the world ought to keep out of the monastery, he may someday come to believe that those in the monastery ought to keep out of the world. Then, the Brothers "would" have a hard time of it.

Barney has another virtue that could not be passed over. He never argues or talks back. He perks up his ears and looks extremely intelligent as he tries to get the meaning of what one says to him. Then he does what he thinks is right.

What is the moral of the story? Perhaps stories ought to tell their own moral, nor need one always moralize. But one truth that occurs is this: that while Barney may never be a good monk, he makes a good dog. One might in a pessimistic mood reflect that it would be better to be a good dog than a bad monk. Or, better, if Francis Thompson dared to refer to Our Lord as "The Hound of Heaven," then we could take delight in referring to ourselves as dogs of the Lord, close to His heels, looking to Him for guidance, awaiting the "touch" of His love, the pat on our heads, accepting His reproofs, showing gaiety in His service and being His glad companions always.

Brothers' Activities

All of the Brothers' activities were going well. The Brothers had a strong presence at Holy Cross Seminary as part of the working staff. They were teaching catechism to many students in the various area parishes. They were well accepted by the pastors and people alike. Brother Charles' crafts were having a spiritual effect on the people who purchased them. Brothers Anthony, Jude and Cletus had the farm operating well, and the print shop was off to a good start.

Brother Edward working at the Seminary

The primary focus, along with all these activities, was the spiritual formation of the Brothers. Each year during the month of January, Forty Hours Devotions took place. Priests from Holy Cross Seminary (Fathers James Coke, Al Thomas, Edwin Thome, Thomas Reardon, James Finucan and John Paul, as well as Bernard McGarty) came to preach, teach and provide spiritual formation for the Brothers. These were special days for the Brothers because they got to know these priests in a more personal way. Many of them were only a few years older than the Brothers. Thus, they had much in common. It also made the Brothers feel a part of the Diocese. After all, they were founded as a Diocesan Brotherhood.

Each summer, the Brothers who were in promises were given the opportunity to make a yearly retreat. Sometimes they would go to the

Trappist Monastery in Dubuque, Iowa; at other times, they would go to Monte Alverno, the Capuchin Retreat Center in Appleton, Wisconsin. On several occasions, a Retreat Master came to De Soto for the annual retreat. One such time was when Father Paul Stimmler, a member of the Sacred Heart Fathers and Brothers in Sparta, came. He began each conference dramatically: "O man, you are a stranger here. Mark it well. You are made by God. You are made for Him. You are made for Him alone." These spiritual exercises, along with daily Eucharist, chanting of the Divine Office, meditation and times of quiet prayer, helped to form a religious spirit within the Brotherhood.

The Brothers also had fun times. Each day after the noon meal and before the 1:15 p.m. None (a segment of the Divine Office), they played volleyball, summer or winter. And quite an exciting game it became. There were no referees, no side boundaries (the walls of the granary and garage were on the sides), and a back line that was a line in the ground. But because they were Brothers, there were never any arguments or disagreements!! In the summer, the Brothers went swimming in the pond along Old Highway 35. They tied a rope to a limb of the tree. Then they took the rope, climbed the slope to the top of the roadside, swung out over the water, hung on for dear life until they were above the water, and then let go of the rope to dive or jump into the pond. Some Brothers made bigger splashes than others!!!

The May, 1957 issue of THE PAX listed the calendar of events as follows:

- Corpus Christi evening Mass and outdoor Eucharistic procession on Thursday, June 20
- Saint Anne's, Saturday, July 27, at 8:00 p.m. with Evening Mass and procession
- Assumption Mass and Harvest Blessing, August 17 at 11:00 a.m. Legion of Mary members have their annual outing
- St. Pius X Feast – Tuesday, Sept. 3 at 8:00 p.m. Evening Mass and Special Homily for peace.

Attendance at these celebrations kept increasing. People loved to come. Members of tour groups were always served a meal, stayed overnight at a hotel in La Crosse, Wisconsin or Lansing, Iowa and returned the next morning for brunch and another outdoor Mass. The Brothers loved these special events, as they fostered a spirit of prayer and devotion. Reaching out to others was one of the purposes of the Community. That was one of the reasons these men had joined religious life.

Brother Francis and Brother Stephen preparing chicken for the pilgrims

Along with the Brothers' successes came difficult moments. Two of the Brothers who were instrumental in erecting the lovely St. Anne Chapel decided that religious life was not for them. Brothers John Resch and Ignatius Riley left the Community. Brother John was one of the two original Brothers who came to La Crosse, at Bishop Treacy's request, specifically to form a new Diocesan Brotherhood. This left Brother Thomas as the only remaining one of the original four. It must be understood that postulancy, novitiate and the years of temporary profession were times of discerning one's vocation. These men, along with all others who left, gave it their best to discover God's will in their life. Then they made the decision to do what they felt God was calling them to do. They were respected for the courage and manner in which they discerned. Their presence was missed.

Father Roemer traveled throughout the Diocese to give talks about the Brothers. Many times, he visited Catholic high schools; at these schools, he would not only talk about vocations but he would perform his magic tricks. He loved to entertain the students in this way, and at the same time, give them an opportunity to think about the vocation to which God was calling them. Brothers Charles or John would accompany him.

Father Roemer performing magic for high school students with Brother John

There were very few parishes in the Diocese that Father Roemer did not visit during the first five years of the Brothers' foundation. His speaking ability and outgoing personality endeared him to the faithful wherever he went. His demanding schedule and responsibility to the Brothers began to take its toll. The stress of constant financial struggles became overwhelming. After a day of recollection at Glen Haven, Forty Hours in Eau Claire and a weekend at Saints Peter and Paul in Wisconsin Rapids, he went for a physical checkup at St. Francis Hospital at the suggestion of Monsignor George Hammes. At the checkup, it was discovered that Father Roemer was totally exhausted from his constant and complete dedication to the ministry for six years. He needed a rest. He spent a couple of months with his family in Wilmette, Illinois.

Upon Father Roemer's return it was decided that a Community council would be formed. Members of the appointed council were Fathers Penchi and Coke, and Brothers Charles, Francis, Thomas and Michael. The purpose of the council was to help with the overall governing of the Community. It was felt that more of the responsibility for the Community should be shared, rather than the entire burden falling on Father Roemer. The function of the council, as stated in the Constitutions, was to be followed.

1958 Candidates

The class of 1958 was fast taking shape. The candidates were:

John McTarsney	Brother Martin	Staten Island, New York
Roger Krentz	Brother Simon	Princeton, Wisconsin
William Eddy	Brother Claude	Waterbury, Connecticut
Arthur Roach	Brother Paul	Eau Claire, Wisconsin

Roger was an organist and joined Brothers Alcuin and Aquinas in playing for liturgical celebrations. John was an artist who did the art work in the print shop as well as designed Christmas cards. William's interest was liturgy. Art had many connections within the Diocese and was a baseball enthusiast. Their talents and skills were used well.

Visitors

Two Church leaders visited the Brothers in the late 50's. The Most Reverend Emmanuel Metaboana, Bishop of Leribe, Basutoland, South Africa came in September. He celebrated Mass in our chapel on the Feast of St. Cyprian, a Bishop in Africa 1700 years ago. The Bishop told us of the resurgence of Catholic life in his country. Before the barbarian destruction, there were 800 Catholic Dioceses in Africa; now, however, there was a great need for priests.

In June of 1959, Alfredo Cardinal Ottaviani, Pro-secretary of the Sacred Congregation of the Holy Office in Vatican City, visited the Brothers. Bishop Treacy brought His Eminence while they were enroute to

La Crosse from Dubuque, where His Eminence had given a presentation at Loras College. In La Crosse, His Eminence was to visit the Franciscan Sisters of Perpetual Adoration. He expressed a keen interest in the Brothers. "The Church," said the Cardinal, "has great need today for Brothers." He was most interested in the catechetical work of the apostolate and expressed the hope that the Brothers would continue to work with much enthusiasm for the greater honor and glory of God, especially in rural parishes where children sometimes were not given the opportunity for catechetical instruction. He expressed his good wishes in the continued development of the Brotherhood.

Alfredo Cardinal Ottaviani's visit with the Brothers in De Soto

Front row: Brothers Alcuin, Michael, Cardinal Ottaviani, William Robert, Paul, Ignatius; Second row: Brothers Bernard, Thomas, Steven, Peter Thomas, Anthony; Third row: Brothers Dominic, Francis, James, Claude, Cletus, Martin, Simon, Matthew

Two ladies who visited often, especially to attend the yearly St. Anne's Field Masses, were Mary Ellen Kelly and Myrtle Jacobson. Both of them were confined to cots. Mary Ellen was from Marcus, Iowa, where she was president of the League of Shut-in Sodalists and published a monthly newsletter called "Seconds Sanctified." Her autobiography was published by Bruce Publishing Company under the title, "But With The Dawn Rejoicing." Her pleasant and outgoing personality endeared her to all who attended the Field Masses.

Myrtle Jacobson had been a friend of Father Roemer when he was pastor at St. Mary's in Viroqua before he became Director of the Brothers. At age eighteen, Myrtle was bedridden. She needed several surgeries just to be able to move her hands and fingers. Despite these handicaps, she did beautiful needlework and her penmanship was remarkable. Little children would crowd around her at the Field Mass because her radiating smile attracted them. Myrtle and Mary Ellen became good friends.

Various groups such as the 4-H Club from Eastman, the Boy Scouts from La Crosse, young couples preparing for marriage, teenage retreatants, the Obrecht Family Orchestra, the boys and girls from St. Michael's Home, the Silver Lining Club, an organization of the Vernon County Shut-ins and students from area parishes came to visit. The Brothers became known for their friendliness and hospitality. The peacefulness of their humble surroundings and the natural beauty of the De Soto area attracted people.

Gardening and Canning

BEANS, BEANS, BEANS! It was canning time in the monastery. Every available space in the yard was used for either a vegetable or flower garden. Frequently after the evening meal, for recreation, it would be announced that it was "PARTY TIME." This meant that everyone would gather to snip beans, peel apples, pick blackberries, clean corn or take care of whatever vegetables were available. The goal was to can enough to feed the Brothers for the winter. With twelve to fifteen young men eating three meals a day, many quarts needed to be canned.

New Candidates, Professions, and Transitions

In 1959, another large group of candidates entered the Brotherhood. These young men were invested with the habit on October 17:

Michael Tierney	Brother James	Independence, Missouri
Ronald Resong	Brother Francis	Neillsville, Wisconsin
Robert Lynch	Brother Ignatius	Chicago, Illinois
Thomas Heber	Brother Matthew	Harvey, North Dakota
James McGinley	Brother Kevin	Gays Mills, Wisconsin

1959 Investiture

L to R: Brothers James, Matthew, Francis, Kevin, Ignatius

A ceremony of profession was held on November 29, 1959, at which fifteen Brothers professed yearly promises. They were Brothers Thomas McAllister, Charles Bisenius, Michael Mandernach, Anthony Gianoli, Edward Zimmer, Stephen Callari, Dominic Nelson, Joachim Welbes, Joseph Lynch, William Robert Ryan, Peter Thomas Henry, Alcuin Beckfelt, Bernard Wavrunek, Paul Roach and Claude Eddy. Brothers Cletus Duellman, Augustine Jira and Martin McTarsney deferred making profession. Bishop Treacy celebrated the Profession Mass and received the promises. Father Penchi gave the homily on *Galatians* 3:27: "You have all clothed yourself in Christ." This put the total membership of the Brothers of St. Pius X at twenty-three.

The year 1960 started off with sadness. Father Roemer's Aunt Martha Busscher died and was buried in Wilmette, Illinois. Martha had come frequently to De Soto. Father attended the funeral, along with Brothers Alcuin and Martin. On January 3, word was received that Father Roemer had suffered a severe heart attack while in Chicago and had been taken to the Alexian Brothers Hospital in Chicago. Father's brother Roland called to inform the Brothers that Father Roemer was in serious condition. An all-night vigil in the De Soto chapel ensued to pray for Father's recovery. Brothers Martin and Alcuin returned to De Soto, while other Brothers went to Chicago to be with Father. This was done on a rotating basis until Father was released from the hospital two weeks later.

After Father was released, he went to stay with Monsignor Urban Baer in Eastman. Dr. John McMahon from St. Francis Hospital in La Crosse became his doctor. On March 15, Father Roemer returned to De Soto. A big welcome-back party was held.

As mentioned earlier, the Colby property transaction took place on December 31, 1959. Brother Thomas took three or four postulants each week to Colby to prepare the house for monastic living. Helping with the remodeling were the class of 1960:

Herbert Schmidt	Brother Raphael	Fort Atkinson, Wisconsin
Wesley Hickie	Brother John	Worcester, Massachusetts
Wesley Hayes		Brooklyn, New York
John Jones		Newton, Iowa

Albert Mozgis		Aurora, Illinois
Arturo Peralto	Brother Xavier	Albuquerque, New Mexico
Forrest Viet	Brother Nicholas	New York, New York
Keith Andersen	Brother Adrian	Green Bay, Wisconsin

All of the plumbing and electrical wiring was replaced. Brother Thomas' parents and friends from Wausau, especially Bud Smith, were a great source of help in this project. The kitchen was enlarged and the whole interior of the house was painted. Two rooms were renovated into a chapel and sacristy. The beautiful walnut paneling of the chapel blended harmoniously with the birch altar and the candlesticks designed by Jerome Krieg, a former member. The Blessed Sacrament was kept in the chapel at all times. Fathers John Pinion, Ambrose Blenker, James Stauber and John Olson, the priests at Colby, celebrated Mass at regular intervals. The renovation project began in the middle of January and, by spring, the Brothers were able to move in. Much hard work had been done on the farm.

Brother Anthony, the farm manager, had the machinery moved to Colby to begin spring planting. Brother Thomas continued to help on the farm. They were assisted by Brother Alcuin, who was the cook and all-around helper. The story is told that Brother Anthony asked Brother Alcuin to let the cows into the barn; it was milking time. Brother Alcuin, like an obedient Brother, opened the back door and, one by one, the cows came in. But they did not go into the stanchions. They walked right through the barn and out the front door, which Brother Alcuin had failed to close. The cows were all on the front lawn eating the luscious green grass. After the roundup of the cattle, all were fine, even Brother Alcuin. "Well," said Brother Anthony, "a young man from the city."

The year 1960 saw the Brothers broaden their catechetical ministry, with Brother Charles and Brother Martin teaching a fifteen-week Catechetical Methods course at St. Wenceslaus Parish in Eastman. The Theology and Scripture were taught by Father Henry Cassidy. Nearly fifty people from the Prairie du Chien Deanery attended. Father Francis Wavra, the Diocesan Director of Catechetics, organized the program and invited the Brothers to teach. It was one of the first such programs sponsored in the Diocese. Brother Charles was the first to be involved in many of our catechetical programs. He was one of the four who began the Summer Vacation Program in McGregor, Iowa. Brother Martin and he were the first

Brothers involved in adult education and, later on, he was one of the two Brothers who began the ministry of education in Catholic Schools.

The catechetical appointments listed in the diary for the fall of 1960 were:

Brother Charles	Hanover, Eastman, Rising Sun
Brother William Robert	West Ridge, St. Philip's, Gays Mills
Brother Michael	West Ridge, St. Philip's, Gays Mills
Brother Dominic	Hanover, Seneca, Rising Sun
Brother Martin	Dorchester, Eastman, Wauzeka
Brother Peter Thomas	Dorchester, Seneca, Wauzeka
Brother James	Hanover, Gays Mills, St. Philip's
Brother Francis	Dorchester, Seneca, Wauzeka
Brother Paul	West Ridge, Seneca, Rising Sun

West Ridge, Hanover and Dorchester were parishes in the Archdiocese of Dubuque, directly across the Mississippi River from De Soto.

General Chapter

In the spring of 1960, it was announced at a council meeting that a General Chapter would be held in the fall for the primary purpose of electing a Brother Assistant to the Director. This would be the first such Chapter held since the foundation of the Community. Father Roemer had appointed Brother Francis Debis and Brother Michael Mandernach to fill that position up to this time. All the professed Brothers were to submit two names to determine the two deputies who would oversee the election. Professed Brothers were eligible to be elected as Brother-Assistant. Brother Peter Thomas Henry was elected to a three-year term. In addition, Brother Edward was appointed superior of the Brothers at the Seminary; Brother Stephen Callari was appointed procurator; Brother William Robert was appointed secretary; Brother Michael Mandernach was appointed farm manager at Colby and Brother Anthony was moved to the Seminary.

Appointments were usually made by a personal letter from Father Roemer. The Rule stated that, "by obedience, the Brothers understand that in a spirit of faith and of love for God's will, they show humble obedience to those in authority, realizing that they are giving service to the up-building of Christ's body according to God's design." (Article 5 in Rule, Constitutions and Directives). It was in this spirit that each Brother received his assignments. Following are two examples of such appointment letters:

Oct. 8, 1957

Dear Brother Thomas,

I am appointing you for another year at St. Michael's Orphanage. You are to be superior of the group of Brothers there. I would like very much to have you exercise your office with prudence, discretion, charity, prayerfully and with the help of Our Lady. I hope that you make every effort to cooperate with the Orphanage and also to uphold the meekness of the community spirit. I, or my representative, will sit down with you and the Brothers in the near future to discuss details of various relationships. Assigned to you will be Brothers Stephen Callari and Peter Thomas Henry. Difficulties may be involved in the living together of only three, but with prayer all should work unto good. I will like you to keep all of the Brothers closely united in spirit with De Soto. The changes will be effective Thursday, Oct 10th. May God bless you and may St. Pius guide you.

Gratefully for the work you have done in the past, I am

Sincerely yours in Our Lady

Very Reverend Albert P. Roemer

The above letter and the following one showed the great sensitivity Father Roemer possessed, as well as his concern for the good of the Community.

Oct 2, 1960

Dear Brother Michael,

First of all, I want to thank you for your labors here on behalf of the Community and your fidelity to religious life. You are appointed to be in charge of the Brothers' House in Colby. It will involve new responsibilities which can be discharged only with the help of God's grace, and it can be only fruitful when done for His honor and glory, the good of souls, and the good of the Community.

New obligations require increased graces; increased graces require greater dependence on God; more humility and firmness of character, total dependence on Christ and steadfastness of purpose.

It will require, too, a firm allegiance to the traditions of the Brothers and association with the center of operations, which is necessary for the direction of the Brothers toward their common goal.

It is not merely the letter of the Rule which counts but the spirit of charity which it is intended to engender. I feel confident that the trials, as well as the joys which this opportunity presents to you, can be the source and growth for you and it can also redound to the good of the Brotherhood.

Sincerely and gratefully yours in Christ,

Reverend Albert P. Roemer

It was in this manner that each Brother received his assignment. Truly, such letters motivated all to do well in their ministry and to take their assignments seriously.

Pilgrims

"BUSLOADS OF INVALID PILGRIMS VISIT DE SOTO," read the headline of the *La Crosse Times Review* on October 21, 1960. Of all the Field Masses held at De Soto and Colby, the ones which hosted the shut-ins and the handicapped had the most meaning. Miss Ceil Tomas of

Minneapolis sponsored a group of one hundred people, thirty-four of whom were invalids of all faiths, most of them in wheel chairs. They came in three buses, arriving from Madison, where they had visited the National Shrine of Our Lady of the Green Scapular.

Busloads of Pilgrims

In his homily that day, Father Roemer said, "Suffering has meaning only in terms of Christ on the Cross and our body at the foot of the Cross. Suffering had little meaning before the coming of Christ and has meaning now only in so far as all the pains of the afflicted were once suffered by the one who was and is both God and man." Referring to the co-workers of Miss Tomas, Father Roemer said, "We do not say thank you for bringing these suffering members of Christ, rather we say congratulations because you have discovered something of the meaning of Christian charity and have put it into practice at a time in history when we and all the world need more of the love of Christ." One hundred pilgrims, a third of whom seldom saw more than the four walls of a room and rarely the beauty of the glorious fall colors on the banks of the Mississippi, returned to their homes in or near the Twin Cities. This event especially made the Brothers' ministry so fulfilling and enriching. Reaching out to God's lovely people helped all to realize that everyone had a gracious and loving God who loved all people.

Divine Office in English

As the Brothers increased in number, the chanting of the Divine Office became more solemn. It was always accompanied by the organ. Father Roemer felt that to chant the Divine Office and to preside at this important function would greatly contribute toward his spiritual solidarity with the Brothers. Father Roemer believed that chanting the Divine Office in the vernacular had fostered a significant movement toward stability and sanctification of the Brothers during the past nine years. This had also helped them in their main apostolic work: the catechizing of children in rural areas. He felt that, in promoting the sacramental and prayer life within the Brotherhood, it would be most helpful for him to be able to chant the Divine Office with the Brothers.

On February 7, 1961 Father Roemer wrote to Bishop Treacy to ask the Bishop to seek permission from the Sacred Congregation of Rites for Father Penchi and him to be allowed to chant the daily Divine Office completely in English with the Brothers. Father Roemer felt he needed to participate with the Brothers during their recitation to ensure regularity in their spiritual exercises and to ensure the proper devout chanting. He thought that presiding at the chanting with the Brothers would fulfill the priest's obligation to pray the Divine Office and it would be of spiritual benefit to both Directors and to the Brothers alike.

Bishop Treacy considered it an excellent idea and turned it over to Father James McDonald, the Assistant Chancellor. Father McDonald wrote to the President of the Liturgical Conference, Father Frederick McManus, for advice. Father McManus recommended that they pursue the request.

Bishop Treacy then formulated a long letter to the Prefect of the Sacred Congregation of Rites, His Eminence Gaetano Cardinal Cicognani, stating his unusual request. In it, he gave a short history of the Brothers, and a summary of their prayer life and their work in catechetics. Specifically, he mentioned that the Brothers had prayed the Divine Office in English from their beginning and that this practice had formed and strengthened their prayer life. He stated all the reasons that Father Roemer had mentioned in his original petition. Then he requested that "The Priest Director and the Assistant Priest Director of the Brothers of St. Pius X be granted the favor of fulfilling their obligation of reciting the Divine Office by saying it in the vernacular (English) in a version approved by the local Ordinary." If permission were to be granted, the Priest Directors would use the same version of the Roman Breviary that had been approved by Bishop Treacy since the Brothers' foundation in 1952.

On April 7, 1961 Father James McDonald received a response from the Sacred Congregation of Rites. He forwarded the message to Fathers Roemer and Penchi: "We regret to inform you that the Holy See has not granted a favorable response." Fathers Roemer and Penchi had received their response. They continued to pray their Breviary in Latin.

Candidates of 1961

Applying for entrance in 1961 were:

Jay Henninger	Brother Conrad	Minneapolis, Minnesota
Michael Hansen		La Crosse, Wisconsin
Fred Weber	Brother Joseph	Mondovi, Wisconsin
Walter Gray		La Crosse, Wisconsin
Eugene Gentile		Hurley, Wisconsin
William Brown		Baltimore, Maryland
James Hornback		New Haven, Kentucky

Only Brother Conrad Henninger and Brother Joseph Weber stayed until the time of their profession. They came to see what religious life was about. Was it for them? Were the Brothers of St. Pius X what they desired? The life of a Brother demanded the ability to be alone as well as to live in a Community. It demanded the development of a life of individual prayer and a desire to share in daily Eucharist and Community recitation of the Divine Office. As any vocation, it had both its challenges and its blessings.

Transition in Priest Directors

On January 6, 1962 the Brothers celebrated the tenth anniversary of their foundation. Bishop Treacy, as always, celebrated this anniversary with Mass, Holy Hour and dinner. He recalled Father Roemer's appointment as

Director and mentioned some of the accomplishments of the past ten years. Weighing heavily on his mind was the health of Father Roemer. Father had suffered a heart attack in 1958. He had carried both the spiritual and financial responsibility for the Brothers. This great amount of stress was taking its toll, emotionally, psychologically and physically.

A year earlier, Father Roemer had asked Bishop Treacy if he could be removed as Father Director, requesting that another priest from the Diocese assume the directorship. Bishop Treacy hesitated to do so; he felt such a move would be a devastating blow to Father Roemer. The Bishop also realized that the spirit of the Brothers had diminished. He did not want that to lessen even more. Father Roemer had instilled in the Brothers a spirit of prayerfulness and a sense of fraternity. They possessed a desire to be of service and an ability to be hospitable and friendly to everyone. They were religious men who provided a welcoming environment and a deep respect for all people. Father Roemer had inculcated in the Brothers a reverent method of liturgical and Eucharistic celebration, what it meant to be a Diocesan Brother and a willingness to do God's will. The Bishop knew that Father Roemer had simply run out of energy. He had given himself completely to God through his ministry to the Brothers. The Bishop knew a change was needed.

The April issue of THE PAX stated: "Father Roemer's fine spirit of leadership and his friendly personality will be missed not only by the Brothers and the people of Sacred Heart Parish here in De Soto but also those who visited us and the many people who had followed the progress of the Brothers in THE PAX and the TIMES REVIEW. His spirit will live on in each of us. In him we have found a true priest of God, another Christ. God bless and keep him." After a period of rest, Father Roemer was appointed pastor of St. John's Parish in La Crosse.

On April 1, 1962 Bishop Treacy appointed Father George Passehl to succeed Father Roemer. Father Passehl's desire from his youth had been to be a teacher. He obtained his Bachelor of Education degree from the University of Wisconsin-Stevens Point, followed by a Master of Arts degree from George Peabody University in Nashville, Tennessee, where he later became a member of the faculty. In 1951, he began his priestly studies at Marquette University and his theological studies at St. Francis Seminary in Milwaukee. He was ordained in 1957. As a seminarian, he was a friend of Monsignor Urban Baer of Eastman and had come to De Soto frequently to visit. At Sacred Heart in Marshfield, Father Passehl formed a boys choir known as the "Singers of the Sacred Heart." His educational interests and background contributed to Bishop Treacy's decision to appoint him as Director of the Brothers.

(L) Father George Passehl, the Second Director
(R) Father Eugene Smith, Assistant Director

Candidates of 1962, 1963 and 1964

During the next few years, more young men joined:

1962

Gerard Schulte	Brother Gerard	Schererville, Indiana
George Griller	Brother David	Sioux Falls, South Dakota

1963

Arthur Brutcher	Brother Kevin	Buffalo, New York
Joseph Kubatska	Brother Gerald	Buffalo, Iowa
Arthur Christensen	Brother Carlos	Owatonna, Minnesota

Anthony Sustarish		White Pines, Michigan
Leland Buchta		Beaver Dam, Wisconsin
Ken Prusik	Brother Andre	Shawano, Wisconsin
Louis Mullen	Brother Fabian	Dougherty, Iowa
Nicholas Shepherd		Michigan City, Indiana
Kenneth Lucas	Brother Paul	Watertown, New York

1964

Kevin Gordon	Brother Kevin	Bayfield, Wisconsin
John Steuck	Brother John	Rudolph, Wisconsin
John Logan		Philadelphia, Pennsylvania
Daniel Kohler	Brother Daniel	Tonawanda, New York
Carl Burger		Worthington, Iowa
Thomas Brinkman		Appleton, Wisconsin

Of the above candidates, Brothers Gerard, Kevin Brutcher, Carlos, Fabian, Paul, Kevin Gordon and John expressed an interest in obtaining an education in either the health care ministry or teaching. It became the goal of the Brotherhood to educate its members to their greatest potential. In that manner, the Brothers would feel that they were contributing to ministry within the Church, that they were an asset to the Congregation, and that this was why God called them to become Brothers.

The Candle Shop

At this time, three Brothers were working at the Seminary and three at the Colby farm. A Candle Shop was opened in De Soto, which required two Brothers to fill the orders received, especially from Marshall Fields in Chicago.

The lively story regarding the Candle Shop was published in the February 1964 issue of THE PAX. BENNY THE BEE, as it was titled, was written by Father Roemer.

Hello, I'm Benny the Bee. I work all day long in the monastery garden, trying my best to be a good bee. It seems that every time I get a little wax Brothers Thomas or Claude come along and snatch it from me. One day I decided that I had enough of this piracy. I gave him a good chase for my wax but decided to see just what he was up to. I immediately flew to the hem of his scapular and alighted there. I was not a bit frightened as we tromped through rooms and passageways. Finally we arrived at the basement room just filled with my wax. I flew about the room and upon adjusting my eyeglasses, I saw a sign saying this was the Candle Shop. So this is where my wax is going. Seeing it was my wax, I have a perfect right to conduct an inspection of the whole area.

On a large table, I saw over one dozen different molds which the Brothers use to make candles. On another table, I focused my eyes on candles that were just being taken out of the molds. I got so engrossed in the works of the Brothers there, that I almost alighted on someone's ear. That would have been terrible. Then I spotted on a shelf the finished products! Never have I seen more beautiful candles. To my astonishment I found that the Brothers use several types of wax. But they keep mine for a special kind of candles, a 100% pure beeswax candle. They make candles for every possible occasion: Baptism, First Communion, Wedding, Anniversary, votive, sanctuary, birthdays, Thanksgiving and Christmas.

Then I remembered, I must be on my way. The Brothers are depending on me. If you ever come to see me, stop in and see the candles.

The Colby farm increased its acreage from 120 to 200 with the purchase of the Matt and Lucille Allar farm. The Brothers felt that, to make the farm more profitable, it had to be enlarged in acreage and stock. The 80-acre farm included twenty milk cows, some machinery, a barn and a house in which the Allars could live. All of the buildings were in good shape.

The Candle Shop and the Print Shop provided supplemental income for the Brothers' education. The Art Shop, too, fascinated people who came for a visit. The glorified Christ placed on either walnut or oak wood, the statues of Mary, the statues of St. Pius X and all the religious art made a wonderful display. Brother Charles directed the Shop and was principal artist, while Brothers Edward and Matthew made all of the wood crosses.

Art Shop display: Brother Charles' plaster work;

woodwork by Brothers Edward and Matthew

Father Passehl often said that everyone was an artist. If life were to be complete, one must create. He told them that the Father Director, Novice Master and all professed Brothers were to mold the novices into the likeness of Christ. If it was fascinating to work with an inanimate chunk of marble, how much more challenging to work with a human being as he struggled from day to day to form himself into the likeness of Christ: to think like Christ, speak like Christ, and act like Christ. As the Brothers worked with novices, they knew that the novices realized, too, that the great work of art was just beginning. It was the Brothers' responsibility and privilege to help these young men to form in their minds a picture of the greatest Brother who ever lived, Brother Jesus.

Brother Charles' greatest interest was in liturgical art. His love for art began at his home. He took an Art Course at Upper Iowa University, where he won awards for his block print design and an original watercolor design. Brother Charles' message to parents and teachers was to encourage creativity. To know how to take the things God created and perfect them further through acts of one's own creativity was what he recommended.

Brothers in Catholic Schools

Bishop Treacy, in selecting Father Passehl as Director, knew that many of the Brothers had expressed an interest in education as well as in the health care ministry. He had seen Father Roemer's emphasis on spiritual formation; now he felt it was time to prepare the Brothers also for their works in the apostolate. Some members had left because they were discouraged lest they never get the opportunity to teach or to minister in other fields. Father Passehl's presence indicated that a change was to happen. Brother Charles was asked to be the substitute teacher of Latin at St. George High School in Lansing, Iowa and Brother Alcuin, the substitute teacher at St. Lucas, Iowa for third and fourth grade students. Brothers Charles and Alcuin's success as substitute teachers inspired Father Passehl to encourage and facilitate the education of any Brother who wished to teach, become a nurse or seek other educational pursuits.

The summer of 1962 found Brothers Charles and Alcuin going to summer school at Upper Iowa State University in Fayette, studying to earn their educational degrees. They had gone to Viterbo College in La Crosse the summer before, probably some of the first men ever to attend that College. Brother Conrad began his studies at Vernon County Teachers

College in Viroqua in the fall. The Brothers' ministry in Education had begun.

Brothers Charles and Alcuin became full-time teachers at St. Lucas, Iowa. Thus, they became the pioneers for the Brothers' future involvement in Catholic schools. Since the beginning of their catechetical teaching, the Brothers believed that the religious and psychological makeup of children entrusted to them would be profoundly influenced by what they taught and how they taught. The Brothers realized that parents were the most important teachers. Until children reached fourth or fifth grade, they mirrored their parents in opinions and attitudes. What the parents held important, the children would also.

Next to parents, the Catholic school teacher and the catechetical teacher possessed a prime position of importance in the religious development of the child. Consequently, all teachers of the Faith needed to be well trained. This training was given to all of the Brothers in their preparation to become catechists, and later, teachers in Catholic Schools, where their influence as teachers of Faith would have an effect in all of their classes.

Brother Conrad continued his studies at Vernon County Teacher's College, Brothers Fabian and Kevin Brutcher attended the University of Wisconsin-La Crosse, and Brothers Carlos, Gerard and Thomas Keilen went to the University of Wisconsin-Marshfield. All of these Brothers attended Wisconsin State Colleges and lived in the Brothers' houses in De Soto and Colby to remain in touch with their religious Community.

As time passed, Brothers Charles, Alcuin, Conrad and Kevin Brutcher graduated, having obtained their teaching degrees. Brother Charles received his Masters Degree in Guidance and Counseling and became the Guidance Counselor at Regis High School in Cedar Rapids, Iowa. For ten years, he was counselor at Regis after being at St. Lucas grade school for five years. Brother Charles became the principal of the Thorp Catholic School system from 1969 to 1971, the first such position held by one of the Brothers of St. Pius X. Brother Alcuin taught five years at St. Lucas, Iowa and then taught at Sacred Heart in Marshfield, Wisconsin. It was from there that he began his studies for the priesthood. He was ordained for the Diocese of La Crosse in 1974.

Brother Kevin Brutcher began his teaching career with the fifth grade students at St. Mary's in Colby, Wisconsin. Realizing that his abilities were more conducive to teaching high school students, he transferred to Columbus High School in Marshfield, where he taught English. After a few years at Columbus, he took a teaching job at Aquinas High School in La Crosse, where he became an award-winning teacher. He went on to get his Masters Degree in Theology at Emmanuel College in Boston.

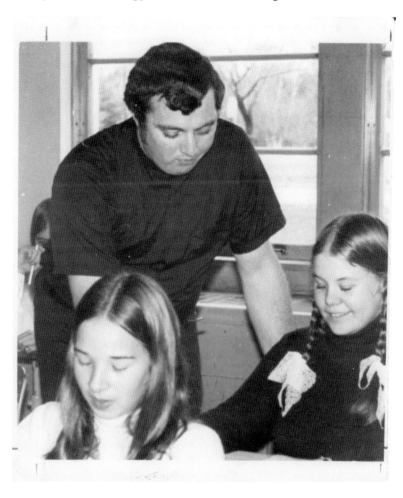

Brother Kevin Brutcher teaching high school students

Brother Conrad taught at Sacred Heart in Marshfield, Wisconsin, St. Lucas in Iowa and at St. Mary's in Colby. His musical and singing talents helped him to become a popular teacher. Brother Thomas Keilen completed one year of college in Marshfield and then pursued a degree in Agriculture at the University Wisconsin-River Falls, where his outgoing personality made him an excellent Resident Assistant.

Teachers learn so much from their students. One incident that could be especially called to mind was the story of the Brother who was teaching the second grade students at St. Philip's in Soldiers Grove. He was telling the students about the presence of God. He said, "God is in heaven, God lives in each person, God is in our beautiful world, God is present in Holy Communion, and God is present in His Word in the Bible." Suddenly, a second grade girl raised her hand and said, "Brother, if God is in heaven, God lives in each person, God is in our beautiful world, God is present in Holy Communion, and God is present in His Word in the Bible, am I not in heaven now?" WOW! What an insight! It was a reminder of John's Gospel alluding to the "already and not yet?" She understood that we already shared in the Kingdom of God and were not yet in heaven. The child's question reminded one of realized eschatology! Yes, out of the mouths of babes!

1965 Investiture

L to R: Brothers Eugene, Richard, Michael, Gary, and James (seated)

Candidates of 1965 through 1975

In the years that followed, some new members also became very interested in becoming teachers. The following list of candidates spanned the years from 1965 through 1975:

1965

Gary Smith	Brother Gary	Cincinnati, Ohio
James Pultz	Brother James	Pavilion, New York
Richard Berendes	Brother Richard	Norwalk, Wisconsin
Eugene Katcher	Brother Eugene	Detroit, Michigan
Michael Neary	Brother Michael	Spring Lake, Minnesota
Thomas Maikowski	Brother Thomas	Milwaukee, Wisconsin
Fred Murray		Shreveport, Louisiana
Francis Stone		Philadelphia, Pennsylvania

1966

Michael Smith	Brother Michael	Menomonee, Michigan
Robert Grams	Brother Robert	St. Cloud, Minnesota
Robert Klabunde	Brother Robert	Wauwatosa, Wisconsin
Joseph Sharp		Springfield, Ohio
Peter Marzen		Stacyville, Iowa

1967

Francis Nitkowski		Portsmouth, New Hampshire
Patrick Pisarek		Necedah, Wisconsin
Louis Jennewein		Patchogue, New York
Robert Julian		Southbridge, Massachusetts

1968

George Viellieux		Somerset, Wisconsin
Daniel Landowski	Brother Daniel	Milwaukee, Wisconsin
Dale Lentz	Brother Dale	North Washington, Iowa

1969

Richard Casola		Rockford, Illinois
David Leos		Carlsbad, New Mexico
Steven Sims	Brother Steven	La Crosse, Wisconsin
John Wech		Lincoln Park, Michigan

1971

Ronald Wendl	Elkader, Iowa

1972

Wayne Truckey	Stiles, Wisconsin

1975

Richard Lerche	Milwaukee, Wisconsin

Of the aforementioned Brothers, Robert Grams, Daniel and Steven became teachers. Brother Robert Grams taught at St. James in La Crosse for a couple of years, before deciding religious life was not for him. Brother Steven had some excellent years in teaching the sciences to students in the upper grades at St. John's in Marshfield and St. Pius X in La Crosse. He had each student display his own wonderful science project at St. John's. The gymnasium was full of these projects and was a wonderful sight to behold. Brother Steven would also judge science projects at other schools. In addition, his ability to play the organ helped to make the children's liturgies, as well as Sunday liturgies, meaningful to all. He played the organ while Sister Sue Kryshak directed.

Brother Steven Sims teaching at St. John's in Marshfield

Brother Daniel teaching at St. Thomas More in La Crosse

Brother Daniel's teaching took him to Our Lady of Peace School in Marshfield and St. Thomas More School in La Crosse. He also taught the upper grade students their sciences. He, too, organized wonderful displays at both parishes. Brother Daniel was an extremely creative teacher who put his heart and soul into his profession. Both Brother Steven and Brother Daniel had the talent of teaching; each student was special and important to them.

Meanwhile, Brother Gary Smith, who for years had been an excellent catechist and the Community chef, was advised to go to school. His Director felt he would make a good Catholic school teacher. Brother Gary's educational experience brought him to Siena Heights College in Adrian, Michigan, from which he obtained his Master of Arts degree in Theology. His first teaching assignment was at St. John's Parish in Marshfield, where he taught religion to the students in the upper grades. His expertise in Scripture and his ability to relate to students then brought him to Pacelli High School in Stevens Point. Brother Gary had the ability to read something and know how to teach it to his students. What a gift!

Sometimes the education of the Brothers would lead them into other areas of ministry. Brother Gerard Schulte, for example, was a catechist, bookkeeper and procurator; he became a tour guide for Pilgrims to the great Canadian Shrines. The April 1969 issue of THE PAX stated:

> For those who are interested in a spiritually stimulating, yet refreshing, and truly enjoyable trip, we sponsor a ten-day Canadian Air Pilgrimage to the great shrines of Canada. We will visit the international and venerable shrines of St. Anne de Beaupre, Our Lady of the Cape, and St. Joseph's Oratory. We will see the quaint, historic Quebec City; as well as the mighty metropolis of Montreal. We are also featuring 'Man and His World,' which is the successor of Expo '67.'

Brother Gerard was usually accompanied by Brother Adrian on these well-loved pilgrimages. Brother Gerard's quiet, knowledgeable and humble leadership was appreciated by all the pilgrims.

Brother Gerard leading pilgrimages to the Canadian Shrines

Meanwhile, even with all of these educational and teaching endeavors going on, the De Soto and Colby houses and the various Community projects still had to be maintained. Brother Steven Callari had been elected Brother Assistant and Brother Thomas McAllister served as Novice Master, both for five years. Brothers Adrian and Paul continued to operate the Print Shop, and Brother Francis and the postulants continued working in the Candle Shop. Brother Dale Lentz, who came from a farm in Iowa, was sent to help in Colby; he eventually became the farm manager, along with Brother Francis Resong.

Additional Living Quarters

Where were all these Brothers housed? In 1958, a residence hall was built in De Soto, with eight private rooms on the second floor, and a kitchen and dining room on the first floor. In addition, in the early 1960's, the Brothers rented what was known as the "Boardman House," where four of them lived. Subsequently, very good friends and neighbors, Dennis and Mae Newton, donated their house to the Brothers. Four Brothers lived there. In Colby, a 40-acre piece of land directly across the street from the Brothers' main house was purchased. This was the Arnold Steinwand property. It had a large brick house, in which, after renovation, six Brothers could live.

Current Events

The Brothers were well aware of the times in which they were living. Some of their priest friends had marched at Selma, Alabama. The Brothers listened to Martin Luther King, Jr.'s famous "I HAVE A DREAM" speech. His assassination stunned everyone. They had also watched the stand-off between Kennedy and Khrushchev in the Cuban missile crisis. Each remembered where he was the day John F. Kennedy was assassinated. For three days, they were glued to the T.V., which they hardly ever watched. Turmoil existed in the United States, and the Brothers remembered the nation in daily prayer.

The Brothers read with delight of Pope John XXIII's desire to begin the Second Vatican Ecumenical Council, and were aware that Bishop John Treacy and Monsignor James Finucan were making plans to attend the First Session of the Council, which would begin on October 11, 1962. These were exciting times in the Church. As Brothers, as catechists, as educators and as members of the Church, the Brothers felt it their duty and responsibility to keep abreast of what was happening in the Church and in the world.

Illness and Death of Bishop Treacy

Bishop Treacy was able to attend the first two sessions of the Second Vatican Council. He attended it with great zest and enthusiasm, as he did all activities. But everyone could tell his health was failing. In the spring of 1964, he sought constant medical assistance. He anticipated a journey to Rome for the Council's third session, but it was not to be. Father Gerald Fisher's account of Bishop Treacy's final months, as recorded in DUST IS MY DAWN, gave us a clue to the Bishop's health.

He had a severe setback on Wednesday, June 10, 1964, and once again he was anointed. Throughout the summer of that year he kept up his spirits, however a circulatory attack on August 11, and a resultant kidney disorder, dimmed his hopes of going to Rome. He spent the last two months of his life confined to his house or at St. Francis Hospital. Death came at 3:30 a.m. on Sunday, October 11. It was the Feast of the Motherhood of Mary.

The Founder of the Brothers of St. Pius X had died. His vision of founding the new Congregation of Brothers had become a reality. Bishop Treacy took time to become acquainted with each Brother. He knew all of them by name. The Brothers attended his funeral and remembered him in prayer.

Bishop Treacy's obituary listed some of his accomplishments. He had established 47 new churches, 47 new rectories, 43 new convents, 42 new schools, a new Seminary and Roncalli Newman Center, a place of worship for Catholic college students in La Crosse. Many words of condolence and honor came from Church dignitaries and civic leaders. The Brothers thanked God for his leadership in the Diocese, for his enthusiastic spirit and never-ending energy, for his foresight in founding the Brothers of St. Pius X and for his faith in God. May he rest in peace!

The death of Bishop Treacy and the resignation of Father Roemer within a two-year period were difficult for the Brothers to endure. They wondered whether they were ready as a small diocesan Congregation to assume more of the responsibility of their own government and leadership. Had they formed a strong bond of Community life, a deep enough prayer life as a Community and as individuals to sustain what lay ahead? It seemed that all the Brothers respected and admired the leadership and work of Father Passehl as their Director. Still, they wanted to move ahead, rely more on one another and become more self-directed. These were good signs.

Bishop Treacy with the Brothers

L to R (seated): Brothers Edward, Thomas, Charles, Joseph, Bishop Treacy, Monsignor Finucan, Brothers Don Bosco, Martin, Michael and John

Back row (standing): Brothers Richard, Francis and Anthony

Most Reverend Frederick W. Freking – Sixth Bishop of La Crosse

On February 24, 1965, the Feast of St. Matthias, Bishop Frederick W. Freking, D.D. was installed. He was born in Heron Lake, Minnesota, and studied at St. Mary's College in Winona. He went to North American College in Rome, and was ordained in 1938. He received his Doctorate in Canon Law, was Chancellor of the Winona Diocese, became the Spiritual

Director at North American College and was named Bishop of Salina, Kansas in 1957 by Pope Pius XII. On December 30, 1964, he received word that he would be the sixth Bishop of La Crosse.

Bishop Frederick W. Freking

In becoming Bishop of La Crosse, Bishop Freking also became the Superior of the new religious Congregation. They looked to him for direction and inspiration. Like Samuel of old, the Brothers said to him, "Here I am." They wanted him to know that they were ready to serve and to help their Bishop. Just as he had roots in the Minnesota soil, so too, the Brothers had roots in the soil. They instructed hundreds of children in rural areas of Wisconsin and Iowa. At that time, they had also made a small beginning as teachers in Catholic schools. They wanted to make every effort to be available to the new Bishop. As loyal Brothers, they would strive to help him to fulfill the goals he set for the Diocese. At the close of each day, as the monastery bell echoed through the hills and valleys calling all the Brothers to chant the Divine Office and to a Holy Hour, they prayed that God would bless Bishop Freking's ministry in the Diocese of La Crosse. The Brothers offered prayers and friendship as the Bishop began his episcopacy among them.

The bell calls the Brothers to prayer

Health Care Ministries

The arrival of Brothers Kevin Gordon, Richard Berendes, James Pultz and, later, Robert Klabunde, Eugene Katcher and John Wech, brought men who were all interested in the ministry of health care.

Kevin Gordon was first. He applied to St. Anthony School of Nursing in Carroll, Iowa, becoming a Licensed Practical Nurse. From there, he attended the Memorial School of Inhalation Therapy in Watertown, South Dakota, from which he graduated with high honors. For the next five years, he worked as an Inhalation Therapist, becoming Director of the Inhalation Therapy Department at St. Francis Hospital in La Crosse. With additional education in administration, he became the Administrator of the Marshfield Clinic in Ladysmith, Wisconsin. Efficient, intelligent, personable, administratively-inclined, patient-aware and health-care conscious, Brother Kevin was well prepared for his ministry. The pastor of Ladysmith thought that Brother Kevin might have a vocation to the priesthood and encouraged him in this regard. Brother Kevin left the Brothers and studied to become a priest for the Diocese of Superior, Wisconsin. He became (and is currently) the Vicar of Clergy and the pastor of five parishes in the Bayfield, Wisconsin area.

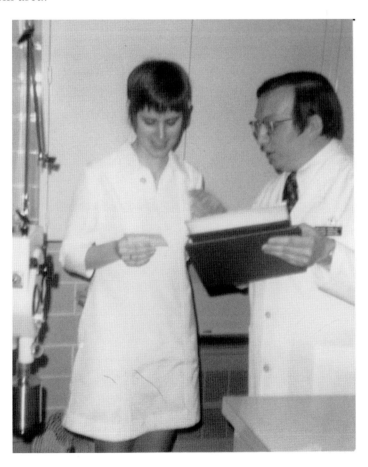

Brother Kevin Gordon, Inhalation Therapist at St. Francis Hospital, with Nancy Bedessem

Brother Richard Berendes helped with many projects around the De Soto monastery. He and Brother Thomas remodeled the Ferryville Post Office and the Arneson Funeral Home in De Soto. Brother Richard then attended La Crosse Vocational School to become a Licensed Practical Nurse. He completed the program and worked for three years in Orthopedics and Urology at St. Francis Hospital, while living at Holy Cross Seminary.

Clockwise from Father Hugh Uhrich: Brothers Richard, Kevin, Adrian and Robert, serving as Extraordinary Ministers of the Eucharist in the St. Francis Hospital Chapel

One morning, while driving down Highway 61, Brother Richard, for no reason whatsoever, was going too fast. Lo and behold! A police officer stopped him. Brother Richard, of course, as a nurse, was dressed in white. When the officer came to his car, he said, "Where are you going so fast?" "I'm going to the hospital," Brother Richard replied. Without further talk, the officer said, "Follow me." The officer turned on his flashing red lights and off he sped. Brother Richard followed him in good speed, but as they were driving down Highway 61, Brother Richard noticed the officer turning off to go to Lutheran Hospital (Brother Richard actually worked at St. Francis). "Oh my," Brother Richard thought, "What do I do now?" The officer drove in front of the hospital and stopped. Brother Richard stopped directly behind him and, thinking quickly, said, "Officer, thank you; please park my car, put the keys in the glove compartment, and I'll get the car later."

That is exactly what the officer did. Brother Richard quickly ran up to the second floor window, watched as the officer parked his car, and then watched as he drove away. Once the officer was gone, Brother Richard went downstairs, found his car, took the keys out of the glove compartment, and drove s-l-o-w-l-y to St. Francis Hospital. With his quick thinking ability, Brother Richard continued his nursing education at Finley Hospital School of Nursing in Dubuque to obtain his Diploma. Brother Richard eventually felt that his calling was not to religious life but to the married state. He married and continued in the nursing profession, first as a staff nurse, and later as a Nursing Administrator with Franciscan Health Care.

The above story was interesting because, in all religious communities, there were some members with character, some members who became characters, and some members who both had character and were funny characters at the same time. That is what made Community life so exciting.

Brothers James Pultz and John Wech became Licensed Practical Nurses and worked at St. Francis in La Crosse and St. Joseph in Marshfield. Neither of them stayed with the Community very long. Brother Eugene Katcher became a nurse also. He worked in the nursing profession for a while before leaving to study for the priesthood. He became a priest (and is currently serving) in the Archdiocese of Detroit. Brother Robert Klabunde became a nurse, too. He worked at St. Francis Hospital in La Crosse and St. Joseph's Hospital in Marshfield. His other great contribution to the Community was his ability to sing and to play guitar. Sisters Marie and Phyllis, Brothers Steven Sims and Robert formed a quartet. They sang for weddings and many other occasions. Brother Robert was especially good in leading sing-a-longs for the Community and visitors. He, too, discerned that religious life was not for him.

Change in Priest Director

The year 1968 saw big changes and challenges for the Brothers. First of all, Father George Passehl, the Director for the last six years, was transferred to Saints Peter and Paul Parish in Wisconsin Rapids on April 2. In his last message in the "Director's Column" of the April 1968 edition of THE PAX, he wrote:

> My six years with the Brothers have been happy ones. Each year has found them growing more and more capable of handling their own affairs. They will soon be out of their teens; they are going on seventeen now. My good friend, Father Roemer, skillfully guided them through their early years. I like to think I took them through adolescence to the threshold of maturity. Like a parent this is the point where I step out.

Father's great influence was that of having each Brother go into the educational field of his aptitude and talent. "Well done good and faithful priest of God." Thank you.

Appointed to replace Father Passehl was Father Albert Raschke, a priest ordained by Bishop Treacy on May 18, 1957. He was assigned to various parishes as Assistant Pastor, most recently to St. Stephen's Parish in Stevens Point. Father Raschke possessed many talents, especially in music. He played the piano and organ well. He was also known as a great debater who loved to challenge other people's thinking. With those gifts, he was to contribute much to the Brothers.

Father Albert Raschke

On October 27, 1968 the Brothers received the shocking news that Father Roemer had died of a heart attack at the young age of 53. His Mass of Christian Burial was at Assumption of Mary Parish in Durand. He was buried next to his parents at the Society of Divine Word Cemetery in Techny, Illinois. His total dedication to God in his priesthood was an example to everyone. His outgoing personality, his great preaching skills, and his gift of forming friendships with all of the Brothers, many priests and lay people endeared him to all. May he rest in peace!

The Brothers' Easter message, drawn by Brother Gary Smith

Renewal and Adaptation

The year 1968 also saw the Brothers begin the program of renewal and adaptation mandated by the Second Vatican Council's decree "Perfectae Caritatis," which called religious to look at their customs, traditions and charisms. Even though the Brothers of St. Pius X were a young Community, they undertook the serious task with full energy and vigor. They understood that the Decree on the Perfection of Religious Life involved two things:

1. a return to the sources of the Christian life and to the original inspiration and charism of their Community,
2. an adjustment of the Community to the changing conditions of the times.

To help with this renewal, Father Jogues Constance, OFM Cap., was invited to be the Brothers' consultant. Father explained the preliminaries of renewal, why communities must renew, why every member needed and was needed for renewal, and the great benefits that would accrue for each person and for the whole Community. Then Brother Stephen, the Assistant Director and leader of the renewal, named the members of the Community's Council who would chair each of the following Commissions:

Community Life	Br. Kevin Brutcher
Spirituality and Personal Development	Br. Charles Bisenius
Apostolate	Br. Michael Mandernach
Formation	Br. Thomas McAllister
Government	Br. Adrian Andersen

The rest of the Brothers, as well as the candidates, were assigned to the various Commissions, so that each Commission had at least four members. Each was to invite a speaker on his area of responsibility to present to the whole Community, and each was to prepare a position paper to present to the whole Community at a Special Chapter in August of 1968.

The plan was that, every August for the years between 1968 and 1975, the Brothers would hold a Special Chapter. In August of 1975, a General Chapter convened to approve "The Constitution and Directives of the Congregation of the Brothers of St. Pius X" as well as the "Rule," which was called "What Love Requires." Father Albert Raschke was a great motivator. He questioned and challenged the Brothers to understand and clarify what the written directives meant.

The first Special Chapter was held at the Christian Renewal Center in Wausau. Mr. William Van Laarhoven, a friend of the Brothers from Medford, was invited to be the parliamentarian. This was the first time the Brothers ever experienced working with "Roberts Rules of Parliamentary Procedures." Mr. Van Laarhoven gave them a few points to remember on parliamentary law. Not too long into the discussion, Brother Edward Zimmer made a statement. Everyone stopped, suspecting that he might be out of order, probably quietly saying to himself, "Thank God, it's not me." Slowly and gently, Mr. Van Laarhoven said, "Brother Edward, you are out of order." Everyone laughed, knowing full well that Brother Edward, the humblest of us all, would laugh with us.

Community Life Commission

This renewal program helped the Brothers to discover the beauty of religious life, the value of a Diocesan Brotherhood and what it meant to be a Diocesan Brother. For seven years, the Brothers prayed, studied, discussed, challenged, laughed, remembered, listened to one another, disagreed and rejoiced. It was all a very enriching and meaningful experience.

Community life was always considered a key component of the Brotherhood. Small buildings and, usually, a limited amount of living space made it necessary for the Brothers to live in close quarters and, most of the time, to live more than one to a room. This did not necessarily mean good Community life, but it forced the Brothers to get to know one another well, as they often rotated living arrangements.

The section of the Constitutions that began the chapter on Community Life quotes from *St. Paul's Letter to the Ephesians* (4:1-3): "Walk in the manner worthy of the calling to which you were called, with all humility and meekness, with patience, bearing one with one another in love, careful to preserve the unity of the Spirit in the bond of peace." The joys of the spirit of togetherness far outweighed the challenges and difficulties of Community living. Brother Gary Smith's humorous yet unbelievable stories, Brother Charles Bisenius' regular recitation of his famous poem about the Maquoketa River, Brother Dominic's imitation of individual Brothers, Brother Kevin Gordon's stories about the hospital environment, Brother

Anthony Gianoli's dressing up as Saint Nicholas and Uncle Sam, the Brothers serving Kool-Aid made from Jello when Brother Stephen Callari came for a visit because they did not have anything else to drink and Brother Alcuin Beckfelt's being surrounded by the ladies coming by bus for the Field Masses were all pleasant memories. After each meal, all the Brothers would do the dishes together. This was always a fun time, because stories of the day were told, gentle teasing and kidding would go on, and fraternity developed.

Article IX of the chapter on Community Life stressed the importance of Eucharistic celebration. It read: "The Eucharistic celebration should be the center of the day, so much so that every action converges on it as a preparation or a thanksgiving. The celebration of the Sacrament of Eucharist should be the daily food which sustains, comforts, and strengthens." A Brother was advised to attend daily Eucharist, if possible.

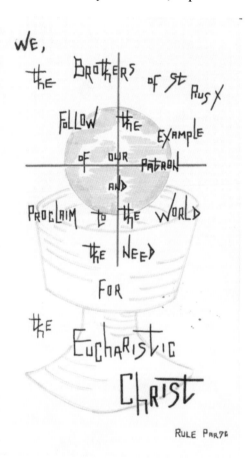

WE,

the BROTHERS of St Rus X

FOLLOW the EXAMPLE

of OUR PATRON

AND

PROCLAIM to the WORLD

the NEED

FOR

the EUChARISTIC

CHRIST

RULE PAR 76

Drawn by Brother Gary Smith

124

During these years of studying Community Life, the Commission decided that those Brothers who had finished their novitiate and had completed three of years of temporary promises would be allowed to make a permanent commitment. It was decided to celebrate that Profession Day on August 21, 1973.

Many people asked why the Brothers of St. Pius X would even think about making a permanent commitment when commitments were fluctuating all around them. Was it precisely because the idea of commitment was being questioned that it would be of value to have religious Brothers live a lifestyle which showed that all commitments and fidelity to those commitments were gifts of God? Yes, the Brothers thought so. To embrace the Lord and His mission in this radical manner was challenging. To follow Him in any kind of commitment, not knowing to what or where it would lead, demanded courage.

The Brothers of St. Pius X believed that, within the Church, there should be a group of men following the path of Christ, exemplifying beautifully what the Church was in its infancy and serving as a model of what the Church could be in the future. They were a small community of men hoping to be a part of a movement within humankind; they wanted to serve, to signify, to liberate, and to anticipate the changes that were to come in the full realization of God's heavenly Kingdom. They believed that they were called to signify and to present to the world, in faith, what the Kingdom of God would be. To give people hope in the Promise of the Kingdom was like incarnating the future now in faith. The Brothers intended to be a sign of the future of human living, and of the faith, hope and love necessary to make it come true.

For this type of community, the Brothers needed to have a strong faith in God. God had to be the reason for their existence. They accepted God as the living force in their lives and in the lives of those around them. In Scripture, they saw a call not only to goodness, but to greatness. If they had faith in God and in people, they had to aspire to holiness. For those who aspired to holiness, as the Brothers intended to do, God demanded everything, including risks. This call to be holy had to be accompanied by a desire to live for others. The desire to serve others required discipline, discipline enough to be a living testimony of faith and redeeming love which showed that they were Brothers living in His presence and "doing what love requires."

Permanent Commitment

It was in this spirit of dedication and commitment that Bishop Frederick Freking celebrated a Mass of Religious Profession at St. Joseph the Workman Cathedral in La Crosse on August 21, 1973. Pronouncing their permanent commitment of the evangelical promises of poverty, chastity, and obedience were Brothers Charles Bisenius, Edward Zimmer, Stephen Callari, Michael Mandernach and Kevin Brutcher. At the same ceremony, Brothers Kevin Gordon, Gary Smith, Richard Berendes, Matthew Heber and Robert Klabunde renewed their annual promises, and Daniel Landowski and Dale Lentz made their first promises.

Bishop Freking receiving permanent commitment of Brother Stephen Callari.

(L to R) Father Thomas Bisenius, Bishop Freking, Father Francis Heindl, Brother Stephen Callari

Formation Commission

In every religious community, the formation process of candidates was a great concern and responsibility. Candidates who desired to become Brothers expected a formation program from the Congregation that prepared them to seek Jesus in the Gospels. The chapter on Formation in the Constitutions began with the Scripture passage from *Ephesians* (5:21, 4:20-24): "Submit to one another out of reverence for Christ. Since you have heard all about Him and have learned the truth that is in Jesus, put off the old man, be renewed in spirit and mind and put on the new person, created in God's likeness, righteous, holy and true."

It was the aim of the formation program to instruct candidates properly according to their intellectual gifts and personal endowments. The program took into account the society in which the Brothers lived. It understood the prevailing manners of contemporary social life, and took into account its characteristic ways of feeling and thinking. If such training were harmoniously coordinated, it would contribute to the integrity of a Brother. Throughout his life, a Brother was to labor earnestly to perfect the spiritual, doctrinal and professional aspects of his life.

Drawn by Brother Gary Smith

The renewal program re-organized the formation program, whereby novices would live at Holy Cross Seminary, have joint classes with the novices at St. Rose Convent, and take courses in Scripture and Theology at Holy Cross Seminary. This seemed to give the novices a much better program than could otherwise be provided.

Some of the goals of the formation program of the Brothers were as follows:

> 1. To provide spiritual growth by exposure to Scripture, liturgy, and dogma to enable a candidate to integrate the spirit of the Gospel into his life.
>
> 2. To insure intellectual growth by providing opportunities for a candidate to develop professionally and culturally.
>
> 3. To perceive the Christian life as manifesting itself in a special way through the practice of the vows.
>
> 4. To become a fully human person who is able to affirm himself as a Religious Brother in such a way that he witnesses Christ and the Christian love in a manner that is Eucharist centered.

All of these beautiful, formative concepts were found in the Brothers' Constitutions; however, one drawback for the Congregation was that those Brothers who were appointed Formation Directors and Novice Masters had not had sufficient theological, Scriptural or religious life education and training. They gave all their energy, doing their best; they had every good intention imaginable in spite of the fact that the necessary qualifications for the job were lacking. The renewal programs that were undertaken helped all of the Brothers to understand more fully what religious life was about, what it demanded, and what it could become. Despite many shortcomings, most of the Brothers would say that their formative years were excellent preparation to live the life of a Brother of St. Pius X. Many former Brothers also said that they were well-prepared for a Christ-centered life outside of the Community.

Apostolate Commission (Ministries of the Brothers)

As mentioned earlier, whenever Bishop Treacy was asked what the Brother's apostolate was, he would respond, "Their works are as broad as the Church." The Brothers were already involved in catechetical teaching, education in Catholic Schools, the health care ministry, working at Holy Cross Seminary, agriculture, printing and Candle and Art Shop work. They served as bus drivers, carpenters, organists, choir directors and cooks; they also organized Field Masses. Through their works in the apostolate, the Brothers touched the lives of many people, especially the young.

At the Special Chapters, the Apostolate Commission recommended that the Brothers broaden the works in the apostolate to make it attractive to new candidates. The Commission believed that the present works were too confining. They suggested that opportunities to work in the Mission Field, such as working with diocesan priests in South America, would expand their service to the poor. The Brothers would, however, remain within the La Crosse Diocesan jurisdiction. Another area to consider would be helping with the Newman Center apostolate as an extension of their teaching efforts. Many of the Brothers had the gift of working with the young to help mold and form the minds of the leaders of tomorrow.

The Apostolate Commission encouraged the education of all Brothers, both those who desired a college education, and those who desired vocational school training in cooking, carpentry or other professions. The Commission warned that the Brothers should keep in mind that their vocation was as a Brother, one who belonged to a religious Congregation; their commitment to the Congregation came first. Their works in the apostolate emanated from their dedication to Jesus as a religious and their commitment to a life of prayer and reflection. "On behalf of Christ, therefore, we are acting as ambassadors, God as it were, appealing through us" *(2 Cor. 5:20)*.

Government Commission

The Government Commission knew that it faced a big issue. Talk in the Community was about the possibility of having a Brother take over the Directorship. For the past fifteen years, the Brothers had been directed by a priest. Some of the Brothers thought that it was time to take the leadership into their own hands. It was not that the Brothers felt the priests did not do a good job. The priests themselves mentioned at times that they felt uncomfortable as Director of a religious community to which they did not belong. Brother Adrian Andersen, the leader of this Commission, realized the challenge which they had to confront.

One aspect of changing from a Father Director to a Brother Director would be the challenge of a Brother being obedient to a Brother Director as he would be to a Priest Director. Any superior would be docile to God's will in the exercise of his office. As a Father Director might look at his community as sons given to him by God and have regard for their personalities, any superior would try to make it easy for all to obey joyfully. Any superior would listen gladly and encourage all to make every possible commitment to his community and to the Church. It was felt that a collegial approach should be used in all positions and jobs. No longer would Brothers just be given a letter of assignment, but all appointments would be discussed with each individual Brother before an assignment was made. The Council suggested that each Brother would have a personal responsibility to express his desires and gifts to the Director.

Discussing the possible change from Father Director to Brother Director required an understanding of these concepts and principles by all of the Brothers. Brother Adrian made a proposal at the August 16-17, 1968 meeting of the General Chapter: "That the Brothers of St. Pius X be governed by a superior, a council, with all professed Brothers meeting in a General Assembly four times a year." Discussion then centered on who should lead the Brothers, a Father Director or a Brother Director. Hours of discussion followed.

Brother Adrian and the members of the Government Commission made the following daring proposal: "I move that the present position of Father Director would become that of an Advisor and Chaplain to the Brothers of St. Pius X." The motion was seconded. It was now on the table for discussion, and discussed it was. Some of the Brothers, many of whom had been with the Brothers longer, felt that, as a Community, they were not able to govern themselves at this time, while others felt strongly that they were. It was debated whether a person not a member of the Congregation should hold the highest governing position within the Community. Also discussed was that if the role of Father Director was eliminated, who would represent the Community to the Bishop? Most believed that a Brother Director could adequately represent the Brothers. It was expressed that the Brothers' associations with all of the Bishops had been excellent. As a Community, they had never given any Bishop any difficulty. Bishop Freking had been delighted to be present at most of the General Chapters.

Father Albert Raschke made a presentation to the General Assembly. With his usual intellectual and philosophical approach, he provided insights regarding both sides of the proposal for whatever direction the Brothers would choose. He advised them not to cut off their life-line to the Bishop. He expressed concern that the relationship with the Bishop and the Diocese would not be the same with a Brother Director as it had been with a Father

Director. However, he expressed his intent, regardless of the direction of the vote, to be there to assist the Brothers as much as he could. The Brothers knew that Father Raschke would keep his promise. He always had been and would be available to advise, provide spiritual direction and celebrate the Sacraments. It was already late in the evening, and the Special Chapter meeting adjourned until the next morning at 9:00 a.m.

After opening prayer on August 17, 1968, Brother Michael Smith, a member of the Government Commission, made the following proposal: "That the present position of the Father Director would become that of a Spiritual Advisor and Chaplain to the Brothers of St. Pius X." It was seconded. Discussion indicated that many felt that the proposal was too similar to the original proposal. A direct quote from the minutes of the Special General Chapter stated: "Finally Brother Michael Mandernach moved to amend Brother Michael Smith's proposal to read as follows: That the role of the Father Director would become that of a Spiritual Advisor and Chaplain to the Brothers of St. Pius X after a period of slowly diminishing responsibilities for one year. His responsibilities would then diminish as follows:

> 1. The Brother Director would be given full responsibility for ordinary Community government.
>
> 2. The Brother Director would approve and sign Council and General Assembly's deliberations before they became effective.
>
> 3. The Father Director would remain as the Community's representative to the Bishop for one year, acting together with the Brother Director."

In addition, at the next meeting of the Special General Chapter the original proposal, namely, that the present position of Father Director would become that of a Spiritual Advisor and Chaplain to the Brothers, was seconded and carried. A sigh of relief went up, since most considered it a compromise proposal acceptable to almost everyone.

Why mention the time and effort spent on this proposal and decision by the Congregation? The readers need to know the time, effort, sweat and blood, anxiety, risk, and hope for the future that went into this endeavor.

Drawn by Brother Gary Smith

The Election of the First Brother Director

Father Albert Raschke was designated by Bishop John Paul to be the Bishop's Observer for the election. Were the Brothers prepared to govern themselves? An election to select the first Brother Director was needed. Who would it be? The day opened with the celebration of Mass and special prayers in honor of the Holy Spirit. This was a time of major decision for the future of the Congregation.

Brother Kevin Brutcher was elected to replace Brother Stephen Callari, who had been Assistant Superior to the Director. Brother Kevin became the Co-Director with Father Raschke, the Director for one year, after which Brother Kevin was to assume the leadership. Brother Kevin grew up in Buffalo, New York and attended O'Fallon High School and Catholic University of America. He came to De Soto in 1963 and professed his first vows in 1965. He was editor of THE PAX, taught CCD and, for three years, was stationed at Colby, teaching fifth graders at St. Mary's School. Elected to the Council to assist Brother Kevin in leading the Congregation were Brothers Conrad Henninger, Gerard Schulte, Robert Grams and Richard Berendes.

In a later issue of THE PAX, Father Raschke made the following comments:

The change from Father Director to Brother Director is desirable because it was the intent of Bishop Treacy in 1952 to start a Diocesan Order of 'Brothers.' Note well the name 'Brothers!' As an order of 'Brothers,' they should have an identity of their own and if this identity is to be real, their direction must be their own. It was a sort of contradiction for the 'Brothers' to have a 'Father Director.'

The first time I wrote for THE PAX in May, 1968, I had indicated that as one grows from childhood to adolescence and from adolescence to adulthood, the needs for guidance and direction change. At that time I saw myself in a transitional role, in which the position of Father Director would become less and less, to its eventual elimination. That day has arrived in the special chapter of the Brothers, when the elimination of the position as well as the title was agreed upon, recognizing by law that which already existed in fact. I will be available to them to help in whatever way I can, to make their new development meaningful and permanent. In the future the Brothers will receive my whole support and be my heartfelt concern.

Change in Habit

Another major decision made during the renewal program was that of a change of the habit. The traditional habit consisted of a black cassock and a green scapular with the green PAX symbol designed through the Chi-Rho on a six-sided black cloth. The new habit approved was the Brother's collar worn with either a rabat or a Brother's shirt. This would be the Brothers' official habit at all formal and special occasions. At other times, they could wear other appropriate clothes. Those who were invested in the original habit could wear it if they so desired. At the ceremony of Permanent Profession, each Brother was given a ring with the PAX symbol imprinted on it. The ring was a sign of permanent commitment.

National Assembly of Religious Brothers

Through the years, many of the Brothers were given opportunities to attend conventions sponsored by the National Assembly of Religious Brothers. It was an opportunity for them to interact with Brothers from nearly forty different religious communities. Brother Damian Carroll, C.P. was one of the originators of these Conferences. Presentations included topics such as prayer, community life and the vows. Discussions and interactions always followed the presentations.

What made these conventions so meaningful to the Brothers was the fact that they learned how other religious communities prayed together, how they lived their community life, and how they ministered in health care, education and other ministries. Meeting other men dedicated in their vocation as Brothers helped the Brothers to appreciate their vocations more deeply. Brothers Michael Mandernach and Gary Smith attended one of these conventions in 1976 in Philadelphia. The convention was held just prior to the Eucharistic Congress, where they heard Mother Teresa give an inspiring talk about "being poor in fact and in spirit."

Brother Kevin's Leadership

Brother Kevin Brutcher's term of office began shortly after the close of the Second Vatican Council. It was a time of religious, cultural and moral uncertainties. Priests, Sisters and Brothers were leaving their vocations for

another calling. The Brothers of St. Pius X had already lost members and wondered what would happen to their small Congregation. During the first ten years, sixty members had joined, but only twelve had persevered. Part of the hope of the renewal process was to engender a community spirit dedicated to God that would bond the Brothers into a true fraternity. They entertained the hope that the renewal program would stabilize the Community.

Brother Kevin Brutcher

Brother Kevin organized a Day of Prayer in De Soto for all the Brothers. Brother Jacques, from the famous Taize Community founded by Brother Roger Schutz, gave the Brothers presentations on prayer, as well as the various forms of prayers used by the Taize Community. Especially meaningful to the Brothers was listening to tapes of the Taize Community praying and chanting.

Brother Kevin was instrumental in forming the Federation of Diocesan Brothers of the United States. At a meeting in Belleville, Illinois in 1969, he was elected Chairperson of the Federation. Five different religious communities of Diocesan Brotherhoods were represented.

Brother Kevin's term of office was both challenging and rewarding.

His dedication, service and ministry during his three years of leadership were appreciated. Brother Kevin Brutcher's three-year term was to expire on August 16, 1970.

Brother Kevin Brutcher and the Council and Committee leaders

L to R: Brothers Thomas, Conrad, Adrian, Gerard, Kevin,
Alcuin, Michael, Edward

The election committee of the Special Chapter scheduled an election for the position of Brother Director. The date for the election was set for May 24, 1970. Father Albert Raschke was again appointed to be the Official Delegate of Bishop Frederick Freking. Each Brother promised under oath to select the member he deemed worthy of the office. A two-thirds majority was required to be elected. Brother Conrad Henninger was elected as the next Brother Director.

136

Brother Conrad Henninger

In the May-June 1972 issue of THE PAX, Brother Conrad wrote the following in the Brother Director column:

Very often on one of our many sunny afternoons or starlit nights, we find ourselves wondering about God, wishing we could see Him. But we don't need to see God to know what He is like. We need only to think about the many things that are like Him.

The sun is like God: it is always shining. It draws each growing thing unto itself and gives it life and strength. Flowers turn their faces toward the sun. Trees stretch out their branches to reach the sunshine and spread their leaves till everyone receives the light. Even on cloudy days we see the sun's light and feel its warmth.

Air, too, is like God. It is all around us. Though we do not see it, we do feel its warmth or coolness. Without air outside us and within us we cannot live. Without God we cannot live.

It's raining while writing these thoughts. The rain reminds us of God's love falling gently upon the earth filling rivers, streams, and lakes. We do not see the rain feeding the roots of plants and helping the seeds to sprout; but we see the grass and fields grow and the flowers blossom. We see God's life in every growing thing.

The bluffs and mountains are like God. They protect families and homes from storms that sweep around them. When we look up at the hills we think about God.

Remember the seas which stretch on and on far beyond our sight. Its surface moves as it wills but deep down it is quiet and still and full of mystery. God is like the sea.

All things beautiful are like God. Special people in our lives are God's most profound way of expressing his being to us. Through their love and in their lives we can see God. Being sensitive to all the wonders about us and in us, we can learn much about God.

The renewal program continued until August of 1975, when the new "Constitution and Directives of the Congregation of Brothers of St. Pius X" were approved and adopted at the General Chapter. At the same Chapter, the Rule: "What Love Requires," was adopted. So concluded seven years of study for the renewal program.

The Death of Father Raschke

On Sunday, August 11, 1974, Father Raschke, who was leader, advisor, guide and friend of the Brothers for six years, was killed in a tragic car accident at the age of 42, near Amherst, Wisconsin. He died instantly. His constant encouragement of all the Brothers, his spirit of hopefulness despite difficult times, both in the Church and in the Community, and his willingness to help in all circumstances, were greatly missed. The Brothers relied on him "to be always there" for them. His death was a great loss for the Brothers, the Diocese and the Church.

3   Decline

Brother Conrad was elected as Brother Director in 1970, but in September of 1972, after much prayer and discernment, he decided to leave the Congregation. Since Brother Michael Mandernach had received the next highest number of votes at the time of Brother Conrad's election, he served as Brother Director for the remaining year of Brother Conrad's term. In August of 1973, Brother Michael was elected Brother Director for a three-year term. Five Brothers made permanent commitments in August of 1973, which was the first year this occurred.

When Father Albert Raschke died in a tragic car accident in 1974, Bishop Freking was given a list of forty names of priests that the Brothers thought would be good chaplains and advisors for them. Quite a few of those priests were in the La Crosse area, and the Brothers knew that they would be good replacements for Father Raschke. The Bishop assigned Father Anton Lecheler to be the new Chaplain and Advisor.

Father Anton Lecheler

These were crucial times for the Brothers. From 1968 through 1976, the following Brothers felt called by God to become priests: Brothers Alcuin Beckfelt, Eugene Katcher, Stephen Callari, Thomas Maikowski, Thomas Keilen and Kevin Gordon. They expressed their desire to Bishops Freking and Paul, and the Bishops approved their decisions. They had been a vital part of the Congregation and had contributed so much. They were greatly missed.

Membership in the Congregation was declining at this time. Accordingly, the Council approved the printing of THE PAX four times a year for two years, and then the publication was terminated in 1977. This decision was made because there were not enough Brothers to work in the Print Shop. All of the equipment was sold, and Brother Adrian, the printer, took a job in St. Francis Hospital's Print Shop.

George Steinwand, the donor of the Colby property who lived with the Brothers for ten years, needed more care. A guardian was appointed for him, and he moved into a health care center in Colby. He was 97. The Brothers who lived at Colby and went to school or taught in Marshfield felt it would be more convenient to live in Marshfield than to drive that 25-mile distance each day. The Council approved their request. And so, the Arnold Steinwand house, the house that had provided housing for the teachers and students who went to Marshfield each day, was sold, and a house was rented in Marshfield. This left just three Brothers working the Colby farm.

The Colby farm was now having difficulty. Brother Dale was really the only Brother interested in farming at this time. Brothers Gerald, Matthew and Ignatius had moved to other jobs. The matter was brought to the Council, which decided that the farm should be sold. When Brother Dale learned this, he requested to leave the Brothers so that he could purchase the farm, along with his mother and his sister's family. (Dale's young father and brother had both died within the past year.) With the approval of Bishop Freking, the transaction was completed.

Within the Church, there was a feeling of, "Where are we going?" Not only had many priests and sisters left their calling, but liturgical and sacramental rites were also in transition. The Vietnam War was still in process, demonstrations were being held in many big cities, and there were riots in the streets of Milwaukee and other cities across the nation. Some fine young Brothers such as Brothers Richard, Robert Klabunde, Gerald, Daniel, Ignatius and Francis left. These Brothers, as well as those who left for the priesthood, had comprised much of the workforce and the backbone of the

Congregation. The remaining Brothers wondered what was happening to their Community.

Brother Michael Mandernach talked with Bishop Freking about what to do. The Bishop, too, felt badly. He could identify with the situation because of the loss of many priests in the Diocese. When Brother Michael mentioned what was happening to Father Cornelius Van der Poel, the priest who had guided the Family Life Program for the Diocese, Father Van der Poel offered consoling words: "Some religious Congregations get their work done in a short period of time."

At one of the meetings of the Congregation, Bishop Freking, who was known to freely share his observations, stated that what was happening to the Brothers would happen to other communities. Their members would also leave and their numbers would decline. Since other communities of religious had more members, however, it would take longer for them to be affected by the decline.

The twenty-fifth anniversary of the Brothers of St. Pius X was in 1977. Bishop Freking came to De Soto to celebrate the anniversary Mass. The Brothers were going through difficult days, but the words of their newly-approved Rule were a reminder of their ministry:

We are a group of men who have been called by God and have freely responded to that call and have dedicated ourselves to the fundamental Christian end, which is the union or fulfillment of all humankind in Christ through the Spirit, giving honor and glory to God the Father.

We hope and pray that through our witness in our varied works we will proclaim and serve God's Kingdom. We strive to live in gratitude and in joy for all we have received, and give thanks, in particular, for the Spirit Who is the bond of our union with God and one another. We respond in thankfulness for every human person, especially our Brothers and all who are our partners in the Gospel.

For years, every Brother needed to work in order to help pay the Congregation's bills. Besides regular jobs, each Brother had to assume responsibilities within the Community, such as Formation Director, Business Administrator or Vocation Director. For example, Brother Daniel taught at St. Thomas More School in La Crosse, Wisconsin and was also Formation Director; Brother Steven taught at St. John's School in

Marshfield, Wisconsin and was the Business Administrator; Brother Kevin Brutcher taught at Aquinas High School in La Crosse and was also the Vocation Director.

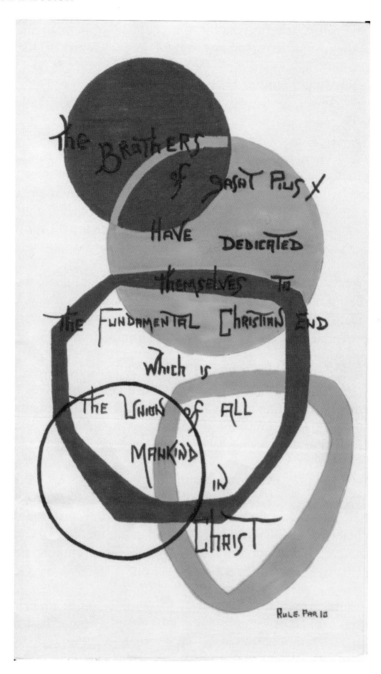

Drawn by Brother Gary Smith

Financially, more money had often been spent by the end of the month than was available in the checkbook. All of the Brothers who had gone to school were appreciative, since the financial support of the Community had helped them to have fulfilling and meaningful jobs working in the Church. Brothers who were nurses brought in good salaries, but some of them had left the Community. Brothers who worked or taught in La Crosse had found it convenient to live at Holy Cross Diocesan Seminary. The Seminary also closed during this turbulent time, so it no longer provided jobs for the Brothers. This left those Brothers who did not go to school or teach without jobs.

The Field Masses at both De Soto and Colby, a source of revenue in the past, were terminated. The Candle Shop and the Print Shop in De Soto had already closed. The question then arose as to what to do with the De Soto property. Perhaps it would make more sense to have the Generalate in La Crosse or in Marshfield where the remaining Brothers were working. The De Soto house was sold, and a house on Winnebago Street was purchased in La Crosse. That house also was sold a few years later and the Trane House on King Street was purchased. This large house made a nice Generalate.

Brother Michael Mandernach had been re-elected as Brother Director in 1976 for another three-year term. At this time, the Brothers of St. Pius X had just two houses, one in La Crosse, Wisconsin and one in Marshfield, Wisconsin. Council minutes from the time reflected feelings of diminished hope. No Brother emerged as a charismatic leader. Was Father Raschke correct when he surmised that, if a Brother Director were elected, the cutting off of the life-line to the Bishop would ensue?

Brother Michael Mandernach

Brother Charles Bisenius

By 1979, Brother Michael Mandernach had fulfilled his two terms as Brother Director, the maximum allowed by the Constitutions. Brother Charles Bisenius was elected to succeed him. Brother Charles had just completed ten years as a Guidance Counselor at Regis High School in Cedar Rapids, Iowa.

After the August 1979 election, the remaining members of the community were Brothers Charles Bisenius, Edward Zimmer, Matthew Heber, Michael Mandernach, Kevin Brutcher, Gary Smith, Steven Sims and Daniel Landowski. The Council decided that all of the Brothers stationed in Marshfield were to discontinue their jobs there, and that one house, the Trane House in La Crosse, would be formed. That house became the Generalate. The Congregation's other properties had already been sold or were in the process of being sold.

Brothers Michael and Steven became the DRE and a teacher at St. Pius X Parish in La Crosse, Wisconsin. Brother Gary Smith began teaching at Pacelli High School in Stevens Point, Wisconsin, and Brother Kevin Brutcher at Totino Grace High School in Fridley, Minnesota. Brother Matthew was taking care of the remaining De Soto property and working in Lansing, Iowa. Brother Charles became a counselor at the Rehabilitation Center for Addictions at St. Francis Hospital. Brother Daniel was seeking a dispensation from his vows, and Brother Edward was attending a nine-month workshop out east.

All of a sudden, some Brothers began to lose hope in that for which they had worked so hard for so many years. The whole renewal program, the writing of the Rule and Constitutions, the hours of study, discussions, presentations by theologians and friendly bantering during those years of Chapters had been successful. The Brothers had felt God's presence in their Congregation. They had listened diligently to the Holy Spirit, Who guided them through the process. They had listened to the Bishop, to their Directors and to one another. But was it enough?

Subsequently, Brothers Daniel Landowski, Kevin Brutcher, Steven Sims and Gary Smith wished to obtain dispensations from their vows, and postulant Richard Lerche decided to leave. They joined the Brothers of Christian Schools. Five great Brothers, five great men, left for an alternative common purpose. Their letters requesting a dispensation told of their appreciation for all that the Brothers of St. Pius X had done for them, how they had grown in their Faith, how they had enjoyed the prayer life, and how they had been successful in their ministries. The one item that all of them felt lacking in the Brothers of St. Pius X was expressed in Brother Gary Smith's letter:

> After further thinking, praying and due consideration, I have decided not to return to the Brothers of St. Pius X. I feel I cannot give the community the total commitment that is necessary. Much of the difficulty lies in the size and mission of the group. I find I could not be happy in a small group. I would also find the one location limiting. Even though I may be free to move about other than the La Crosse house, I would have to live alone or with another community.

> At this time I desire to belong to a larger community with many houses and ministry opportunities within the community. By "mission" I refer specifically to the diocesan emphasis. I would like to move beyond the diocese of La Crosse in ministry and living situations.

> My future plans are to become a candidate in the Christian Brothers. I am grateful for all the Brothers of St. Pius X have done for me. My growth in the community has been extensive and fulfilling. The community has given me much and I am very thankful.

The same sentiments were echoed in all five letters. Bishop Freking was contacted by members transferring to other Communities. He approved their dispensations from the Evangelical Counsels.

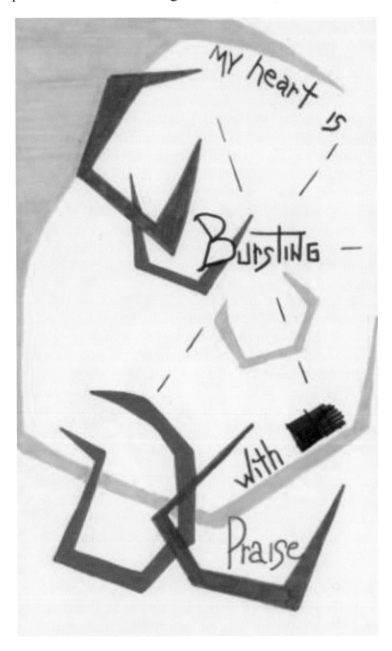

Drawn by Brother Gary Smith

With only four remaining, Brothers Edward Zimmer and Matthew Heber felt there was no hope for the Brothers of St. Pius X's survival. They requested a dispensation from Bishop Freking. It was granted for them to return to the lay state. Again, two outstanding men who had given so much to the Congregation had left. Brother Edward continued working at Viterbo College in La Crosse and Brother Matthew returned to North Dakota. All of them, those joining the Christian Brothers and the others had given many years of service to the Brothers of St. Pius X. Brother Edward had given over thirty years; others had given up to twenty years. A bond of friendship and fraternity had been formed. Only Brother Charles Bisenius and Brother Michael Mandernach remained.

Brothers Edward and Matthew

The Directive: A Bitter Pill

In August of 1982, Bishop John Paul requested a meeting with Brother Charles and Brother Michael. He asked that they prepare a financial report of the Brothers for him to review. This they did. After looking at the financial report, he discussed the future of the Brothers with them. They talked about various options that might be employed for the regeneration of the Brothers. Should they begin anew? Should they become a "Pious Union?" Brother Charles thought that they were too old to begin anew. Finally, Bishop Paul then recommended that they not accept any new candidates and that the two remaining Brothers continue as they were. When they died, the Congregation would cease to exist.

After their meeting with Bishop Paul, Brothers Charles and Michael were returning to Westchester, Illinois, where Brother Charles was the Guidance Counselor at St. Joseph's High School. Both Brothers were in shock about the Bishop's request that they not accept any more candidates.

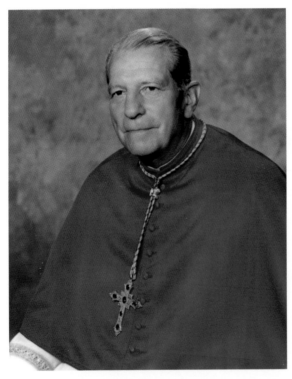

Both had given thirty years to the Congregation; for their efforts to end so abruptly was a bitter pill to swallow. Were those thirty years of hard work, prayer and discernment "down the drain?" What could have been done differently? How much of the blame for the Congregation's eventual demise might be their fault? Both had had leadership roles. Both had entered near the beginning of the Congregation in 1952. It was a long ride that day. Brother Michael returned from Westchester to attend St. John's School of Theology in Collegeville, Minnesota.

Bishop John Paul, 7th Bishop of the La Crosse Diocese, native son, known to the Brothers from their foundation

Two Brothers: A Contrast

A review of the years between Bishop Paul's directive that the Community not accept new members and Brother Charles' death painted a different picture of the lives of Brothers Charles and Michael. Brother Charles' and Brother Michael's journeys for the next thirty years were significantly different. These years found Brother Charles more engaged in his profession and drawn always more toward his Iowa home. Brother Charles' religious life was marked by the years he spent outside the Diocese of La Crosse. Brother Michael, on the other hand, pursued additional education in pastoral ministry and accepted assignments from the Bishops of La Crosse in parishes throughout the Diocese.

A sharp contrast between the lives of these two men as religious Brothers also became apparent. Charles chose to live out the remainder of his religious life in the comfort of his family home, working as a grade school counselor for several Catholic Schools in the area, and being available to his siblings until their deaths. Brother Michael, by contrast, remained in the Diocese of La Crosse, and continued to make himself available to serve. He was responsible for closing and then for selling the property in De Soto, which was expensive to maintain and time-consuming to sell.

A clearer picture thus emerged of the response of the two remaining Brothers subsequent to Bishop John Paul's 1982 decision regarding the future of the Brothers of St. Pius X. In the absence of a Community of Brothers, Brother Michael embraced more fully the "community of the faithful" under the direction of the Bishop, living out his life meeting the pastoral needs of several parishes in the Diocese of La Crosse, where he has been well-known and well-loved for the past six decades.

Brother Charles Bisenius

Charles Bisenius had joined the Brothers of Pius X from Cascade, Iowa. Charles was one of three children, all of whom entered religious life. His sister, Eleanor, a Sister of Charity of the Blessed Virgin Mary, was educated as a physical therapist and worked in Dubuque. His brother Thomas was a priest for the Archdiocese of Dubuque, Iowa.

Charles was the youngest and most outgoing of his siblings. He was the life of a meal or party; he could entertain and loved to do so. He was full of stories, anecdotes and music. Charles had a short repertoire of songs he could play on the piano, but he played with both flair and gusto, leaving his audience to believe he knew much more than he did. He was very talented artistically in both music and the fine arts, but he seemed easily bored and distracted with his tasks, assignments and locations.

Charles was an early member of the Community. He received his formation in De Soto, Wisconsin, along with the other original Brothers. Life on the River was perfect for Charles; he loved the water, the opportunity to be outside and the camaraderie of the young and growing Community. Charles had zest, whether for entertaining, cooking, or preparing and participating in the Eucharist and the Divine Office. His assignments as a young Brother found him teaching CCD (catechism classes) in various parishes in rural Vernon and Crawford Counties in Wisconsin and Allamakee County in Iowa.

Brother Charles' first assignment away from the motherhouse was to work with the boys at St. Michael's Orphanage in La Crosse, where a group of Brothers had been assigned for several years. After that assignment, Charles returned to De Soto to direct the Liturgical Art Shop. At that time, he also taught Latin and religion at St. George High School in Lansing, Iowa.

From 1963 to1969, he and Brother Alcuin taught in the Catholic grade school in St. Lucas, Iowa. Young students loved Charles' energy and imagination in both his approach and classroom presentations. His classroom was full to overflowing with objects to enhance learning, from an aquarium to a terrarium and beyond. One might be overwhelmed by the sights and sounds of his classroom, but generally, a visit made one wonder what else he had in there, and what was new. Pastors, parents, students and his fellow Brothers all appreciated Brother Charles' approach, energy and creativity in classroom decor and presentation.

While teaching at St. Lucas, Brothers Charles and Alcuin attended night and summer school classes to complete their undergraduate degrees. Charles received a BA in Education with a minor in History from Loras College in Dubuque, Iowa. From 1969 to 1971, he was principal and administrator of Thorp Catholic School in Thorp, Wisconsin.

Charles then became the Director of Guidance at Regis High School in Cedar Rapids, Iowa, a position he held from 1971 to 1979. He continued his education at the University of Northern Colorado in Greeley, receiving a Master of Arts Degree in Psychology and Guidance/Counseling. During this period, Charles forged many relationships and renewed old bonds with priests, religious, family and friends in the Archdiocese of Dubuque. He fostered and nourished these relationships for the remainder of his life, always seeking reasons to return to his beloved Iowa.

Following his time at Regis High School, Brother Charles accepted the Community's call to leadership as Director of the Brothers from 1979 to 1982. This proved to be interesting and sometimes challenging for both Charles and the rest of the Community. For a dozen years, Charles had not lived in community with the Brothers, so the day-to-day experience was unique. Most of these men had never lived with Charles, nor he with them; personal habits required adjustment on the part of all in such close living arrangements. The challenges of communal living, including sharing meals, praying and respecting space without isolating people, all required attention.

Communication was essential to success; so was consensus. There were elements of consensus-building in the role of Brother Director, which were all new to Charles. His great skill for hearing people at a deep level was countered by his great reluctance and difficulty in sharing his own self at that same level, possibly because of his time away from the group, or possibly because of his professional background as a counselor. Added to this was the newness of the role of Brother Director and the reforms happening within the Community. Charles was happy to see his term as Brother Director completed.

After this term, Brother Charles became the Assistant Director of Halfway House Federation of Wisconsin in La Crosse. Working with people with addictions seemed more in keeping with his professional training and personal preference. In 1982, when Bishop Paul curtailed the acceptance of any new members, Brother Charles had already signed a contract to be a counselor at St. Joseph's High School in Westchester, Illinois, a school operated by the Christian Brothers. He remained there from 1982 to 1984. Brother Charles continued his tradition of using the summer months for summer school and personal travel. Following his time at St. Joseph's, he took a position as School Counselor at Notre Dame High School in Niles, Illinois from 1984 to 1988.

Brother Charles retired to his ancestral home in Cascade, Iowa in 1988. He died there on March 14, 2012 and was buried on St. Patrick's Day, March 17, next to his parents Raymond and Sarah Bisenius and his brother

Father Thomas. At Brother Charles' funeral, Father Douglas Loecke celebrated the Mass of Christian Burial and delivered the reflection to the many friends of Brother Charles who were present. Father Loecke told the story of one of his experiences with Brother Charles. He was invited by Brother Charles for dinner.

Brother Charles asked him, "What do you want to eat? Do you like steaks?"

"Yes," Father Loecke said. "I love steaks."

"And what kind of steaks do you like?" Brother Charles asked.

"Oh, about any steak will do, but I especially like tenderloin," Father Loecke responded.

"And how do you like to have them cooked?" Brother Charles wanted to know.

"Somewhat rare, about between rare and medium," Father said.

"That shouldn't be too difficult to do," Brother Charles responded. "But, Father, you know just what kind of steaks you like and how you want them prepared. Why don't you pick up the steaks at the grocery store, bring them over on Sunday evening about five. You can cook them as you like them and we'll have a good time together."

Everyone laughed, as all knew this was a typical Brother Charles episode.

Brother Michael Mandernach

Brother Michael joined the Brothers while they were still living in their first home in La Crosse. He helped move the Brothers to De Soto on July 4, 1952. He was there to paint, to dig trenches, to build the chapel and to work at all the many other activities. He worked at Holy Cross Seminary, taught catechetics in over twenty parishes and served as Brother Assistant for five years. Then he spent nine years as farm manager at the Brothers' farm in Colby.

He attended the Formation Director's Program at Aquinas Institute in Dubuque, Iowa, after which he became the Community's Formation

Director. He took an active part in the Renewal Program and in the General Chapters. He also served as a table recording secretary for two La Crosse Diocesan Synods.

Brother Michael served as Director of Religious Education (DRE) at St. John's in Prairie du Chien, Wisconsin and St. John's in Marshfield, Wisconsin. His ability to relate to people, especially to the young, made him an effective teacher and Director. Brother Michael completed three wonderful years as the CCD Coordinator at St. Pius X Parish and School in La Crosse in 1982. He had learned so much from the pastor, Father William Grevatch, the principal, Sr. Louise, and the school's dynamic faculty. The teaching staff at the school combined both the spiritual and academic aspects of the curriculum. The CCD staff was well-trained, well-prepared and well-intentioned to teach the youth of the parish. The parish liturgies, with its multiple choirs, the parish outreach programs, and the parish's fun gatherings, such as campouts, the celebration of Seder meals, and the deep expression of prayer and faith of the members, made it a parish "pleasing to be at."

Brother Michael felt fortunate to be accepted at St. John's School of Theology in Collegeville, Minnesota, since he was already 53. The first morning at breakfast, a young seminarian asked, "And what do you teach?" Smiling, Brother Michael said, "I am a student like you." Brother Michael gave it all he had. Brother Michael's experiences in various jobs before going to the School of Theology helped him to understand the Theology and Scripture courses. He had taught these truths in class, he had experienced them in religious life, and he had witnessed them in the lives of students and parishioners.

With professors like Fathers Godfrey Diekman, Allan Bouley, Jim Urbanic, William Skudlarek, Jonathan Licari, Michael Kwatera, Sister Doris Murphy and others, he was like a sponge. Such courses as Patristics, Liturgical Rites, Sacramental Theology, Homiletics, Catechetical Methods and Christology kept him not only busy but excited and interested in learning. However, he worried about his grades. The first time he had an exam in Fr. Allan's Liturgical Rites class, a brilliant young deacon sitting next to him received his exam back, for which he had received a C+. "Oh, my God, this is going to be the end of me!" Brother Michael thought. When he received his exam back, he opened it carefully and slowly. When he saw a B-, God and all the saints were thanked, and he realized that he would be able to hang in there with this wonderful group of young deacons and seminarians.

Part of the program at St. John's was an eleven-week course of studies called the "Jerusalem Program." Students were invited to go to Jerusalem, to live at a Franciscan Monastery in Ein Karim, to travel to the holy sites in Israel, to climb Mt. Sinai in Egypt, and to visit cities such as Bethlehem and Jericho. Brother Michael's good friend and roommate, Norb Gaier, and he had dinner on July 4, 1983 at King David Hotel in Jerusalem. The experience of praying at the Mount of Olives, the Holy Sepulcher, the Dome of the Rock and so many other sites enriched their faith. The reading of Scriptures became much more meaningful.

Brother Michael's next stop in 1984 was as CCD Director at Roncalli Newman Center in La Crosse, Wisconsin. After receiving his Master of Divinity Degree, he felt, for the first time, adequately prepared for his job. The Newman Center was a parish and church for the students from all public colleges in La Crosse. Father James Mason was the pastor, Sister Kathleen Adams, the campus minister, Pat Topel, the secretary, and Brother Michael the Religious Education Director. The staff included a Father, a mother, a Sister, and a Brother. This did not happen too often! Brother Michael enjoyed the college environment and the experience of both the Newman Parish and the University faith community. About four times a year, the Men's Choir from the University would sing at the Sunday Mass to enhance the liturgy. Hundreds of students came to Roncalli for Sunday evening Mass. Their faith and their presence were admirable.

Brother Michael could have stayed at the Newman Center for years, but one day, as he was coming back from the Newman Center to Holy Cross Diocesan Center where he lived, Bishop John Paul stopped him and asked if he wanted to be the Pastoral Associate at Sacred Heart Parish in Spring Valley and St. Luke's Parish in Boyceville, Wisconsin. This was exactly the position Brother Michael had hoped would someday come his way. This was the opportunity! However, he had only been at the Newman Center one year. What would Father Mason say? Bishop Paul said that he would take care of Father Mason and that Brother Michael should think about it. He told Bishop Paul the next day that he would love the position. Bishop Paul told him to contact Father George Becker at Elmwood and Father Vaughn Brockman, who was pastor at both St. Joseph's in Menomonie and St. Luke's in Boyceville. Brother Michael knew Father Brockman from his days at Holy Cross Seminary, and he knew that Father Brockman and Father Becker were considered excellent pastors. Brother Michael had taught CCD for Father Becker at St. James in Rising Sun, Wisconsin years before. Fathers Becker and Brockman, who possessed such keen insights and perspectives on things, were both a joy to work with.

156

Above: Br. Michael with Father Bill Neis enjoying a famous potluck dinner

Below: St. Luke's Church at Boyceville

Brother Michael was assigned to be in Spring Valley on July 9, 1985. He arrived at 7:30 p.m. because he knew there was an 8:00 p.m. council meeting, at which he would meet the parish council members. In his heart, he knew that they were somewhat disappointed that they were not assigned another priest. This was the first time in seventy-five years that the parishioners did not have a resident pastor. He had received a call from Bob Richardson when he was still at the Newman Center, welcoming him to the parish. This gave him the encouragement he needed. Brother Michael had always been fairly good with names, and so he made every effort to get to know people's names.

Father Cook with lay ministry program's ceremony at
St. Joseph's Cathedral

L to R: Bob Richardson, Bill Crownhart, Father Robert Cook, Father
George Becker and Brother Michael Mandernach

Father Varkey and Brother Michael with the parents of baptized infants

Father Brockman invited Brother Michael to tour St. Luke's Parish with him. When they visited, he met Joe Pieters, who was painting the dining room, and Amanda Zirgible, who was a fifth grade student living across the street from the church. It was at this time that each parish in the Diocese was to organize a parish council with several committees: Worship, Education, Social Justice and Family Life. Each parish was also to have a Finance Council and committees for Buildings and Grounds and Cemetery. These consultative councils and committees were to give the pastor the assistance he needed. Quickly they learned what the word "consultative" meant. They were very helpful to the pastor, but the council members found out that the Church was not a democracy. Just because they might vote overwhelmingly for an issue did not mean the pastor was necessarily required to accept their advice. But they also found out that the pastors did listen to them, and that they were appreciated by him as well.

Another thing mandated to each parish was the writing of a "Mission Statement." With input from many parishioners, this process allowed people to express their faith and their vision of what parish life and ministry were all about; most of all, the process gave parishioners a chance to talk about God, the Sacraments and who Jesus was in their life.

It was an exciting time in Brother Michael's life, too. RCIA programs, Bible Studies, adult education, along with very strong CCD programs, an excellent choir at St. Luke's, two excellent choirs at Sacred Heart (adult and youth) and liturgies at both parishes that helped enrich the life of the parishioners were a plus. Fathers Becker, Varkey and Louis rendered powerful homilies at Sacred Heart. Fathers Brockman, Slowiak, La Porte and Neis preached the Word of God well and encouraged the parishioners at St. Luke's to apply the messages in their lives.

Brother Michael had many good times in the parishes: weddings, Baptisms, First Communion Masses, Confirmation Masses, Holy Week services, Word and Communion Services, potluck dinners, St. Luke's Annual Bazaar, Sacred Heart's St. Pat's Dinner, the 25th Anniversary at St. Luke's, the 125th anniversary at Sacred Heart, Vacation Bible Programs at both parishes and Youth Rallies at Round Hill. He admired the participation of students attending Steubenville North and the students helping at Caring and Sharing Hands, as well as the students helping the people at St. Luke's paint the outside of the church.

One of Brother Michael's greatest joys, especially during his "younger" days, was his involvement with youth. What a gift and a blessing of God parents have in their children! Brother Michael marveled when he witnessed the Baptisms of the children. At St. Luke's one nice Sunday morning after Mass, he saw little two-year-old Leah Adams. He took her hand, and they walked outside around the church. She talked; he listened. He talked; she smiled. When they got back, her folks were surprised that she was not afraid. Another time at Sacred Heart, Brother Michael was teaching the Juniors and Seniors a marriage course. On a piece of paper, they were to write their five best personal qualities. Right away, one girl said, "Oh, I'm a good basketball player." Brother Michael said, "That is a talent. I want you to think of your best qualities, such as a being a kind person." "Oh," she said. Later, when he read her paper, she had written, "I'm honest; I tell it as it is." Then in parentheses she put "KINDLY." Brother Michael laughed. The young were so precious to him.

The Ecumenical Thanksgiving celebrations and the monthly ministers' meetings helped develop friendships with ministers of other faiths. Brother Michael cherished many friendships with the Catholic people of both areas, but with people of other faiths as well, and enjoyed meeting them at the Post Office or on the streets.

There were also times of heartache and tragedy. The fatal heart attack of a man in his 40's and the death of a young man of 49 who died of cancer were sad events. Another was driving with Father Varkey to a hospital in the Cities at 10:00 p.m. to anoint a young man 16 years of age who was scheduled for surgery. There was also the grieving with parents over the loss of a 20-year-old son in a car accident and also of another son, who, at 42, died of heart failure. Often Brother Michael grieved with families on the occasion of the death of a parent, always praying to God for the grace to say the right prayers, to speak words of comfort, and just to be present.

One of Brother Michael's papers at St. John's School of Theology was entitled, "Pastoral Presence." Now, he was given the chance to practice the ideals he had expressed. Little did he realize the strength and power of being present to people in a pastoral setting. While making Thursday morning Communion rounds in both parishes, he witnessed the faith that people had in the Real Presence when they received the Body and Blood of Christ. Visiting with them and listening to the expressions of their faith were mutually gratifying. He felt that all of these people were much more present to him than he could ever have been to them!

During the years between 1994 and 1996, Brother Michael was appointed by Bishop Paul to minister with Father Leon Powell at St. Anthony's in Cazenovia, St. Mary's in Keyesville, Sacred Heart in Lone Rock, and St. Kilian's in Bear Valley. These small parishes were at the southeastern end of the La Crosse Diocese. The opportunity to teach again in a small Catholic school, St. Anthony's, presented itself. St. Anthony's School was a small school with a delightful principal and unique staff. One day a father of two boys in the school noticed that a beaver had built a dam across a small river. He brought a tractor and hay rack to the school. All of the students hopped onto the hay rack and then rode off to view the beaver and dam. The students learned about God's beautiful creation of animals and nature. Every parish and every school had a spirit all its own. Brother Michael could identify with those four rural parishes, inasmuch as they were similar to the one in which he had grown up.

During these years, Brother Michael needed to spend time in De Soto to sell the Brothers' remaining property: a house and two empty lots. Maintaining this property was costly. It took some years to sell all of it. While in the process of selling, Brother Michael worked in religious education programs in neighboring parishes and taught in the RCIA program at St. Charles in Genoa. So many of these people he knew from the early days in De Soto, at which time they had been extremely generous to the Brothers.

Following the sale of the De Soto property, the people of Sacred Heart Parish in Spring Valley invited Brother Michael to return there. He chose to accept the invitation and provided parish ministry to Spring Valley, a community at the northern edge of the La Crosse Diocese. Brother Michael ministered a total of seventeen years in Spring Valley, nine of which included parish ministry in Boyceville. His ministry lessened in late spring of 2013 with the assignment of Deacon Kevin Ray to the three area parishes of Spring Valley, Boyceville and Ellsworth. Brother Michael used this time in 2013 to mid-2014 to move to the Holy Cross Diocesan Center in La Crosse to complete the writing and editing of this book. He then returned to Spring Valley, to minister in a more supplemental capacity.

In the history of the Brothers of Pius X, Brother Michael remembered very few times that a pastor, an employer, a principal, or any other person in authority complained about the work of a Brother. It seemed as if God had prepared them for whatever ministry they would be called to perform. One ministry seemed to make them ready for the next. Fortunately, the scandals that have rocked the Church in the past decade were not visited on this Community.

Raymond Leo Cardinal Burke with Brothers Charles (L) and Michael (R)
at Our Lady of Guadalupe Shrine

Bishops Burke and Listecki

During the nine years that Bishop Raymond Burke was Bishop of La Crosse, he participated in two reunions. At the first reunion of the Brothers of St. Pius X in 1999, which would have been their 47th anniversary, Bishop Burke expressed thanks for the Brothers' years of ministry. Nineteen current and former members were present. In August of 2002, he celebrated the 50th anniversary of the Brothers of St. Pius X at Holy Cross Diocesan Center. The chapel was filled with current and former members of the Brotherhood, along with their relatives and friends.

Bishop Burke then arranged a six-month sabbatical for Brother Charles to study Scripture and Theology in Rome. It was a great opportunity for Brother Charles to visit all the religious sites of Rome, as well as the historical ones. Both Brothers Charles and Michael were invited to visit with Bishop Burke often. In fact, he frequently invited the Brothers to confer about their ministries and their personal lives.

During his nearly five years in La Crosse, Bishop Jerome Listecki also invited both Brothers to the Chancery Office. He was particularly concerned about their physical and spiritual well-being. Brother Charles was living in his family home at this time. Brother Michael was still on the staff at Sacred Heart Parish in Spring Valley. Both Bishop Burke and Bishop Listecki manifested a genuine spirit of concern and care for the two remaining Brothers.

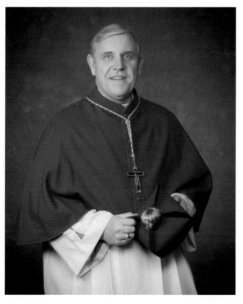

Bishop Jerome Listecki

4   Brothers Together

Who Were These Men We Called "Brothers?"

Recognition needs to be given to those men who were with the Congregation for at least a year and gave so much to the development, the life and the spirit of the Congregation. These are the men who carried out a lot of the "behind the scenes" ministries. They were the ones who taught countless students in CCD classes. They are the ones who spent time planting the garden, milking the cows, getting ready for the Field Masses, chanting the Divine Office, cooking the meals and doing the other one hundred or more jobs. A thank you is owed to them for being part of the Brothers of St. Pius X, even if just for a short period of time.

In giving a capsuled history of these Brothers, two symbols: and ✝ are used. The PAX represents a permanent commitment to the Evangelical Counsels of poverty, chastity and obedience, while the cross ✝ symbolizes being deceased. The Brothers are listed in the order of their arrival.

BROTHER THOMAS (Donald) McALLISTER - Brother Thomas, along with Brother John, was instrumental in the foundation of the Brothers of St. Pius X. Brother Thomas' dream of a diocesan religious Brotherhood became a reality. His dedication and his desire to do whatever it took to get the Congregation started were greatly admired. No job, no task, no challenge, no obstacle was ever too big for him to tackle. Whether it was the remodeling of the De Soto property or the Colby farm house or barn, Brother Thomas was always up to the task. Whether it was organizing the Colby bazaar, planning the Assumption Harvest Field Mass or opening the Candle Shop, Brother Thomas entertained no hesitation or doubts. Sixteen years of his life were given to the Brothers. He is faithful in attending the reunions. His ownership of two religious goods stores, one in Fargo, North Dakota, and one in Sioux Falls, South Dakota, keeps him constantly in touch with vessels of the Church and things of God.

BROTHER JOHN (Marcus/Mark) RESCH - A barber, a builder, a boxer, a butcher, a boiler room worker and a baseball enthusiast was Brother John. He and Brother Thomas McAllister were the first two members of the Community. During the year 1954, Brother John worked at Holy Cross Seminary and tended the boilers. He cut up the first beef that the Brothers butchered. The steaks and hamburgers were luscious! He was foreman for the building of the Brothers' St. Anne Chapel in 1955. All of the Brothers looked neat because of the excellent haircuts that Brother John gave them. After nearly six years in the Congregation, he left and continues to work as a barber in Wausau, Wisconsin. Mark has come to the reunions of the Brothers of St. Pius X. The dedication to the Eucharist that he practiced as a Brother is still manifested today in his daily life with his wife and family.

BROTHER FRANCIS PETERS - This handsome, jovial and delightful young man, not quite 18, with his melodious voice not only provided harmony to community singing, but also blended in well with community life. He was talented in carpentry, along with a willing heart to do whatever needed to be done. He realized shortly after his arrival, however, that he was called to the married state. The spirit of the Brothers has remained with him. He makes the PAX symbol with honey on his cereal each morning at breakfast, stating that his cereal tastes better that way.

BROTHER MICHAEL MANDERNACH See previous narrative in Chapter 3.

BROTHER DON BOSCO McDERMOTT This affable, skinny young man of just 18 had a great desire for things of God. His prayerful spirit added much to the Community's prayer life. He cooked many a meal for the Brothers with his cooking talents; he became famous for his "whole wheat bread." After he left, he kept up the spirit of brotherhood by forming his own Congregation, "The Brothers of Our Lady of Peace," who now serve in Thailand. He used a smaller version of the symbol of the PAX for their habit.

BROTHER ANTHONY (Ralph) GIANOLI ✝ No one ever had a more hearty laugh than Brother Anthony. He played St. Nicholas and Uncle Sam on various occasions. His training on his family farm in Genoa, Wisconsin served him well. He became the Brothers' farm manager, both in De Soto and Colby. He was a favorite with the priests and students when he worked at the Seminary. Every Congregation needs a "Brother Anthony" to help build a spirit of fraternity and delight. His joyful personality brought happiness to all he worked with, especially his family after he left the Brothers. He met a tragic death when he was murdered in his own home. How sad to see the life of such a humble, quiet, happy and peaceful man end so tragically!

BROTHER CHARLES BISENIUS ✝ See previous narrative in Chapter 3.

BROTHER MARTIN (Jack) HIGGINS ✝ Jack had one year of education at Loras College in Dubuque, Iowa and had a desire for more schooling. He worked diligently at Holy Cross Seminary in the boiler room and scrubbing floors. Jack left after he realized that it would be a few years before any of the Brothers would be going to school. He had a prayer room in his family home because he appreciated the spirit of prayer he had experienced as a Brother. Jack and his wife were killed tragically in a car accident.

BROTHER RICHARD DELANEY ✝ This young man must have had angelic wings, as he climbed on top of an altar in an abandoned area church to tear it down so that he could rebuild it to make an altar for the first Field Mass in De Soto. He also was one of the first four to catechize in McGregor, Iowa. There, too, he climbed the altar to decorate it for May Crowning. Because of his admiration for Father Roemer and his spiritual experience while with the Brothers, he studied and was ordained to the priesthood, and was able to stand before the Altar of God each time he celebrated Mass in the Diocese of Monterey, California.

BROTHER FRANCIS (JOHN) DEBIS ✝ A veteran of World War II, Francis experienced a typhoon while serving near Japan. He had grown up in Staten Island, New York before coming to the little town of De Soto to join the Brothers. He ministered at Holy Cross Seminary for three years as secretary to the Rector, Father (later Bishop) John Paul. He was very exacting in all his work, and he did a lot of it. All the Brothers have remembered the famous toboggan ride, in which they coaxed Brother Francis to take the first seat on the toboggan. About a foot of new snow had fallen the night before. This was the first ride, and it was a long one, down the bluff. Poor Brother Francis wore glasses, and by the end of the ride, the snow was packed behind his glasses so tightly that he could not see. He quickly caught on when everyone began laughing that he had been tricked. He missed the big city and returned to New York.

BROTHER EDWARD ZIMMER ✝ This humble man with the big eyebrows was affectionately known as "Steady Eddy." He learned the Hail Mary with the words "pray for us Zimmers" instead of "pray for us sinners." His ministry brought him to work at Holy Cross Seminary for seven years, the farm in Colby for eight, some years at De Soto, with the remainder spent on the maintenance staff at Viterbo College. Brother Edward loved to work with wood. He made the wood crosses created in the Brothers' Art Shop in De Soto and while working at Viterbo he repaired anything made of wood that was broken. He said the longest it ever took him to make the Stations of the Cross was two weeks. (He erected a set of outdoor Stations in De Soto). Brother Edward gave thirty-three years to the Brothers before leaving the Community. A good man of God!

BROTHER STEPHEN (William) CALLARI ✝ His mother and priest brother brought Bill to De Soto in the spring of 1955. Bill liked what he saw and stayed for almost 20 years. He served the Community as Procurator, Brother Assistant, Bookkeeper, Catechist, Cook and in other positions. He and Brother Adrian served many a feast of spaghetti and meatballs as well as chicken cacciatore. His schooling took him to the University of Detroit to obtain a degree in Religious Education. During all his years as a Brother, he assumed leadership roles and had responsible community positions. He felt called to become a priest, was ordained for the Diocese of Marquette, Michigan, served as a Newman Center pastor as well as a pastor of parishes for over twenty-five years.

BROTHER DOMINIC (Jack) NELSON ✝ This man brought many a laugh to the Congregation. He was a funny, mischievous, handsome story-teller and was delightful to have around. He loved to mimic celebrities, especially Red Skelton, and of course, the Community's Directors and Brothers. He spent hours in the Print Shop printing THE PAX and all the other printing orders. Many times he worked late into the night to complete work that needed to be done. Jack was an only son and felt a responsibility to his family, so he left. What he learned in the Print Shop, he used in the Art Studio at Mayo Clinic as a Graphic Illustrator. Jack had a great devotion to St. Pius X until he died in 2004.

BROTHER JOACHIM (Melvin) WELBES ✝ A man of deep prayer, Brother Joachim brought a reverence and an appreciation for the Mass that helped all of the Brothers to participate in the Eucharistic Banquet with deeper understanding. He could recite all the prayers of the Latin Mass by memory. Holy Cross Seminary benefitted by his work there. He hailed from Wausau, Wisconsin and returned there after six years with the Brothers.

BROTHER JOSEPH (James) LYNCH - Small in stature but big of heart, Brother Joseph came to us from Wichita, Kansas. He was an excellent CCD teacher, proficient in cleaning, and a lover of music, all of which made him a valuable asset to the Congregation. He and another Brother accompanied a pregnant Native American woman to a Prairie du Chien hospital, arriving just in time for her delivery. Brother Joseph talked to her all the way, hoping that she would not deliver until they got there. He must have said a few prayers on the way too, because they arrived at the hospital just in time. When he left the Community, he returned to Wichita, Kansas.

BROTHER WILLIAM ROBERT (William) RYAN – Brother William grew up in the Queens section of New York City. Accordingly, he had quite a shock when he came to the little town of De Soto. Since he had never lived in the country before, he thought that Brother Anthony should give the cows feed of more substance than hay or oats, something like steaks! He became very popular with his CCD students. He had never driven a car before coming to Wisconsin and became a good driver. He saw God in the created beauty of the lakes, rivers and bluffs around De Soto. In time, he returned to New York.

BROTHER AQUINAS (Joseph) GREEN - Brother Aquinas helped all the Brothers to praise God better by providing wonderful organ music for the chanting of the Divine Office and celebration of Mass. He was another one of the "funny" guys who could entertain during recreation time with his "You wouldn't believe" jokes. He called St. Louis, Missouri home, and when he came to us, he could not get over how small the monastery was. His contributions to the Brothers were certainly significant, even though his time among us was relatively brief.

BROTHER PETER THOMAS (James) HENRY - This talented young man with a great personality came from Norwood, Massachusetts. In 1960, he was the first to be elected to the position of Brother Assistant to help Father Roemer guide the Congregation. Among all of the Brothers, he was one of the favorite teachers. His talent was admired by all the pastors. He ministered at St. Michael Home in La Crosse, Wisconsin taking care of the boys in the upper grades. His radiant smile brought joy to all and gave the message: God loves you; smile! After several years, he returned to Massachusetts.

BROTHER JUDE (John) ALVIN ✟ Brother Jude was a strong Packer fan from the Richland Center, Wisconsin area! As a young person he thought about the priesthood, but chose the brotherhood. This strong young man had a zest for life and participated fully in the prayer life, work life and play life of the Brothers. His stay was relatively brief, but the effect of his time with the Brothers affected the rest of his life. He never missed a reunion. His involvement in his parish included being an Extraordinary Minister of Holy Communion in his parish and also to the people in prison. Brother Jude was known as the gentle giant who was a big hugger. At his funeral, his three children mentioned how much John loved his time with the Brothers and what it had meant to him.

BROTHER ALCUIN (John) BECKFELT - This red-headed young man from Grand Rapids, Minnesota possessed an outgoing personality. He was not afraid to get involved in any activity. His organ-playing skills enhanced the Brothers' worship of God; his cooking skills fed their bodies; his teaching abilities in both Catholic schools and CCD programs educated many students; and his delightful spirit endeared him to all. His love for God was reflected in all that he did. God's love for him was shared with people through laughter, fun and concern for others. His desire to be a priest had been with him since his youth, and he pursued that dream. He left the Congregation, studied for the priesthood and was ordained in 1974 for the

Diocese of La Crosse. He served for over thirty years as a pastor and as a hospital chaplain.

BROTHER BERNARD WAVRUNEK ✝ Coming from a close-knit family such as Brother Bernard's helps one live a life of faith. His dependence on God gave him a spirit of friendliness and reliance on the gifts that God gave him. His willingness to work on the Colby farm, even though he grew up in the city of Neillsville, Wisconsin showed his willingness to do whatever he was asked to do, and he did it well. Brother Bernard enjoyed company because he loved to entertain. He especially beamed when the Notre Dame Sisters from Neillsville, Wisconsin came. Giving them snowmobile rides, and sometimes pretty fast ones, delighted his heart. Eventually he returned to Neillsville.

A Christmas Card designed by Brother Martin McTarsney (1953)

BROTHER MARTIN (John) McTARSNEY ✝ The second member from Staten Island, New York was a talented young artist who provided many of our Christmas card designs, cartoons in THE PAX, and decorative designs for candles. Brother Martin's contemplative spirit inspired all the Brothers to be more reflective in their daily living. His teaching skills made him one of the more sought-after CCD teachers by pastors. The enthusiasm for the things of God that he developed while with the Brothers for six years never left him. A few years later, through the encouragement of Brother Charles, John studied to become a priest and was ordained for the Archdiocese of Dubuque. He became known as an excellent preacher. Unfortunately, he became ill and died at the age of 61.

BROTHER PAUL (Arthur) ROACH - Brother Paul grew up in the city of Eau Claire, Wisconsin watching Hank Aaron and Billy Bruton play baseball for the city. Baseball remains a big part of his life, even to this day. Brother Paul's time with the Brothers was brief, but he described his stay this way: "The memories of each one of the Brothers I knew still remain special to me after all these years. I miss the Breviary and the walks up the bluffs. I have learned over the years that you can take the man out of the monastic setting, but you cannot take the monastic concepts out of the man." He was an x-ray technician at Northern Center in Chippewa Falls, Wisconsin for thirty years.

BROTHER SIMON (Roger) KRENTZ – "Sing a new song to the Lord (*Psalm* 149)" comes to mind in thinking of Brother Simon. He was an extremely talented organist who could get a lot of music out of a little Baldwin organ. His playing accompanied the singing of the "Salve Regina" each evening at the close of the Holy Hour. This young man had many gifts and he went on to use them well for the glory of God. His time with the Brothers helped him to be successful in life.

BROTHER FRANCIS (Ronald) RESONG - Music was also the talent of Brother Francis. He not only played the organ but the accordion as well. His um-pah-pahs rang out through the bluffs of De Soto and across the Mississippi River. His design talents were used well in the Candle Shop as well as at Christmas time flocking trees. He was so good that his nickname became "Franny Flock." His willingness to serve anywhere brought him to be superior at Colby. Brother Francis especially remembered the swimming hole where the Brothers took a rope and then dived into the pond. To this day, Ronald uses his organ talents as the organist at St. Mary's in Neillsville, Wisconsin.

BROTHER IGNATIUS (Robert) LYNCH - Coming all the way from Chicago, Brother Ignatius grew up in an orphanage and spoke glowingly about the kindness of the Sisters there. His quiet demeanor, his gentle spirit and his kind treatment of everyone served him well in his job at Holy Cross Seminary. The priests and students loved him and his work. This native of Chicago adjusted well to the farm in Colby, where he kept the lawns and flower gardens looking beautiful. He returned to a hospital in Chicago to work for the Sisters.

BROTHER MATTHEW (Thomas) HEBER - Brother Matthew spoke glowingly about the prairies of North Dakota where he came from, especially the city of Harvey. He attended one year at St. Mary's University in Winona, Minnesota and knew the Brothers there. Brother Edward and he made a wonderful team of wood-workers in the Art and Carpenter Shops. His easy disposition and his prayerful attitude served him well while he worked at Holy Cross Seminary and the Colby farm. He looked after the De Soto property just before it was sold and loved working in the lumberyard in Lansing, Iowa. After his departure, he nurtured his prayer life by attending daily Mass and making rosaries.

BROTHER XAVIER (Arturo) PERALTO ✝ This excellent cook provided "spice" in the Brothers' lives, preparing tastier meals than they were used to. His Spanish background and growing up in Albuquerque, New Mexico told him that "hot peppers" and "chili powder" were necessary ingredients in all foods. Slowly he learned, and the Brothers adjusted to "moderately spiced food." Brother Xavier was a big help when the Colby property was being prepared. His willingness to clean, scrub and paint made the Colby farm house, with its lovely chapel, a place of deep pride. He ran a wonderful Spanish restaurant in Albuquerque after he left.

BROTHER NICHOLAS (Forrest) VIET - Brother Nicholas has kept in touch with the Brothers these past fifty years through e-mails and phone calls. Of all the men who had been with the Brothers, Brother Nicholas remembered so many small details. He remembered Father Roemer's wonderful classes and the beautiful chanting of the Divine Office. He liked to remind Brother Michael that he was the oldest of the Brothers at age 31. He especially remembered the life-style lived by the Brothers and the small monastery buildings compared with those of most religious orders. This young man from the big city of New York appreciated the time he spent in De Soto because it helped his faith life, which has remained strong to this day.

BROTHER ADRIAN ANDERSEN ✝ Adrian joined the Brothers from the village of Howard, Wisconsin near Green Bay. He had a keen interest in the arts and music, and was also an excellent cook. His deep and still presence served him and the Community well. Brother Adrian directed the operations of the Print Shop, which was a bustling business that was frequently understaffed and that had equipment far too small for the task required. Even with those limitations, orders of excellent quality were delivered on time. He enjoyed people and was enjoyed by them. On several occasions, Brother Adrian joined Brother Gerard and supported pilgrims on visits to the shrines in Canada.

BROTHER CONRAD (Jay) HENNINGER - This young man from Minneapolis possessed a gracious personality and was one of the first Brothers to enter the educational field. Sacred Heart School in Marshfield, Wisconsin, St. Mary's in Colby, Wisconsin and St. Luke's in St. Lucas, Iowa were schools that benefitted from his presence. Along with his teaching skills, he played the guitar and had a wonderful singing voice. He served the Community in various positions, one of which was second Brother Director. He served as Director for two years and then discerned that God was calling him to the married state. He enjoyed the liturgies and prayer while with the Brothers. His teaching in Catholic schools and CCD and having been given the opportunity to go to school were highlights for him; they prepared him to teach in parochial schools for over forty years after leaving the Brothers. The greatest legacy he received while with the Brothers was "taking care of God's people."

BROTHER JOSEPH (Fred) WEBER – This young man from Mondovi, Wisconsin, was probably one of the most prayerful of all the Brothers. He had a loving heart, a deep desire for community and a willing spirit. No job was small, no task was unimportant, and all work was to be pleasing to God. He learned to be a good cook and served a lot of meals at Colby, finding out very soon that "farm Brothers" were big eaters. Brother Joseph loved the Field Masses and all Masses celebrated anywhere. To listen to Brother Joseph lead the rosary was a religious experience in itself. After Fred's leaving, he encountered some health issues and was also in a serious car accident. His cheerful disposition and his strong faith in God help him to live each day with joy and hope.

BROTHER GERARD SCHULTE - "Still waters run deep" is an expression that fits Brother Gerard. One would never find him loud and boisterous. This soft-spoken man had gone to Holy Cross Seminary in La

Crosse and saw the Brothers working there. His coming to De Soto to join them was truly a gift to the Brothers. He was good with details and served as bookkeeper and accountant. The students in his CCD classes loved him. They knew that they would never be yelled at, and they knew that they would be well-taught and loved. Brother Gerard's great desire was to lead pilgrimages to the shrines of Canada, and that he did many times. His knowledge of these shrines was vast, and pilgrims loved the tours. His talents were missed when he left. He was an accountant at a hotel for many years.

BROTHER KEVIN BRUTCHER Brother Kevin held many community positions, from Vocation Director, Formation Director, Editor of THE PAX to Brother Director, besides being an excellent teacher at both the grade and high school levels. He used his degree in English well by writing some of the position papers for the Congregation's Special and General Chapters. During his days as Brother Director, he led the challenge of the Brothers' preparation of the Rule and Constitutions. Any student who had had him in class knew immediately that he was a firm and fair teacher. His sense of humor kept the faculty members where he taught waiting for a surprise at any time. One of his messages in THE PAX said, "During this month of November, when we remember those who have gone before us and when we set aside a special day of Thanksgiving, let each of us resolve to carry on the tradition of our forefathers and be thankful for all we have. Each day, try to find something for which we are thankful. Most often, a thankful person is a happy person, a positive thinking person is a happy person, and a smiling person is a happy person." Brother Kevin joined the Christian Brothers in 1981 and remains with them to this day.

BROTHER GERALD (Joseph) KUBATSKA ✝ Simplicity of heart is a gift of God not every person possesses. That described Brother Gerald very well. He loved the simplicity of the De Soto monastery and he admired the beauty of the Mississippi River and the De Soto bluffs. The area reminded him of his days growing up in Buffalo, Iowa. Cooking was one of the gifts he brought to the Community, and he used it well. He cooked for the Janus Lodge in Davenport, Iowa after he left. Joseph's deep faith and his dedication to prayer was a trait that his wife Rayneld admired in him. Joseph's death in 2012 was a shock to everyone.

BROTHER PAUL (Ken) LUCAS ✝ Many hours of Brother Paul's ministry with the Brothers were spent running the printing press. He, along with Brothers Dominic and Adrian, took seriously their responsibility of printing THE PAX, THE VOICE OF PEACE, and all other orders. Being a CCD teacher was a great joy for Brother Paul. Teaching that "God loves all," and that his students were to love God in return brought joy to his heart. Brother Paul sought a religious community that was larger and had other various apostolates. He eventually joined the Presentation Brothers in Canada.

BROTHER KEVIN GORDON - Kevin came to the Brothers from Bayfield, Wisconsin with a great desire to be a servant of God and to minister within the Church. His skills led him into the health care ministry while he was with the Brothers. His discipline in studying and his ability to learn quickly were two gifts God gave him. Serving as an Inhalation Therapist at St. Francis Hospital in La Crosse and as an administrator in the Marshfield Clinic in Ladysmith, Wisconsin are two examples of the positions he held. He felt called to the priesthood and was ordained for the Diocese of Superior. Father Kevin now serves as Vicar of Priests in that Diocese as well as pastor of five small parishes.

BROTHER THOMAS KEILEN - This extremely intelligent young man from New Richmond, Wisconsin, the fourth oldest in a family of ten, grew up in a faith-filled family. Attending Mass and family prayer were part of Tom's life as a young boy. He immediately fit into the catechetical apostolate by teaching CCD in local parishes around De Soto. After his formative year, he was appointed to work in the agriculture apostolate and attended school at the University of Wisconsin-River Falls. There, he was a member of the dorm council and always had an "open ear" for the students. He was often asked what his secret was in being a Christian. He usually smiled and said, "There is no secret--all one has to do is to live one more day, just one more day for God and smile; but you must remember to smile." He left the Community to study for the priesthood and was ordained for the Diocese of Superior.

BROTHER GARY SMITH ✝ Brother Gary joined the Brothers in the spring of 1965, the youngest of three sons of Martha and Harold Smith. He came to the Community as a trained catechist, having been trained, along with his mother, in his home parish of St. Theresa's in Union City, Pennsylvania where the catechetical program was managed and staffed by the Victory Knoll Sisters of Huntington, Indiana. The Victory Knoll Sisters were dedicated to parish work, with attention to the religious formation of the young. In addition to his passion for education, Brother Gary was passionate about food; he trained as a chef with the Franciscans in Cincinnati, Ohio. He was also an accomplished, self-taught artist. Several examples of his work appear in this book. He was a man of multiple talents, boundless energy, keen interests, possessing a strong voice and a large physical presence, which made Brother Gary an entertainer and a force to be reckoned with.

BROTHER RICHARD BERENDES - This small town man from Norwalk, Wisconsin has made it big in the nursing profession. After the completion of his novitiate, he and Brother Thomas used their carpentry skills to remodel the Post Office in Ferryville and the Funeral Home in De Soto. Brother Richard's dream was to get involved in the health care ministry, which he did by taking LPN courses at Wisconsin Technical School. He worked at St. Francis Hospital for a few years and then realized that, as a Registered Nurse, he could do so much more. It was then that he went to the Finley Hospital Program to become an RN. He was a man who possessed a mind with a magnificent perspective on life and other matters. He and the Brothers knew that he would make a good nurse. He had a marvelous and extremely successful career as an administrator of the Long-Term Care Services and as an administrator of all the Nursing Home Health Care Centers belonging to Franciscan Skemp Health Care.

Brother Richard Berendes as a nurse with Mrs. Louise Ender and her daughter Mary Jo

BROTHER THOMAS MAIKOWSKI - Milwaukee was where Brother Thomas grew up. He had a great desire for education and became a substitute teacher at St. Lucas, Iowa soon after he came to De Soto. His passion for knowledge and facts as a teacher included his desire to study theology and Scripture. His thinking followed that of St. Jerome: "To be ignorant of Scripture is to be ignorant of God." In talking to his spiritual director, he soon realized that God was calling him to the priesthood. He was ordained for the Diocese of Gallup, New Mexico, where he served as Director of Education for many years. He has also served as the principal of a Catholic high school.

BROTHER ROBERT GRAMS - Brother Robert was in the first class of the post-novitiate group to join the Franciscan Sisters of Perpetual Adoration Formation team and the Formation team of the Brothers of St. Pius X for classes and dialogue. At the same time, he taught at St. James School in La Crosse, since he possessed a college degree before he came to the Brothers. Being a little older than the other members of his class, Brother Robert brought a certain maturity and seriousness. He was all business as a teacher. His students did well in his classes, for which he was very proud. Brother Robert was elected as a Council member early in his religious life. He returned to St. Cloud, Minnesota after five years with the Brothers.

BROTHER ROBERT KLABUNDE - "Smile and the world smiles with you" typified Brother Robert. His gentle, kind and dynamic personality made him a favorite wherever he ministered. He brought joy and delight to all with his melodious voice, ability to play the guitar and leadership in directing groups in song. Brother Robert took delight in the numerous times each day that the Brothers came together for prayer, and that they took time out to do so. He enjoyed being the Vocation Director and going to parishes to speak about the vocation of a Brother and the Brothers of St. Pius X. Going on walks with the other Brothers to enjoy the scenery of the Mississippi River and the bluffs is a memory which has stayed with him. His time with the Brothers has helped him in living his Christian faith and expressing his vocation to his marriage. His ten years with the Brothers helped him to become a caring, loving individual for the sick in his profession as a nurse. Bob says that he and his wife now participate in prayer groups and many religious activities: "My former life as a Brother of St. Pius X has provided me with the background needed to live a good Christian life and share the experiences with my family."

Brother Robert and his parents at his investiture

BROTHER DANIEL LANDOWSKI - Large in stature, big in heart, gifted with talent and a great desire to give of himself in ministry, Brother Daniel inspired all of the other Brothers to come to appreciate their vocation more deeply. He used his natural gift as a teacher well. His input at the General Chapters through his writings, verbal presentations and insights was a major contribution making those Special and General Chapters such a success. Brother Daniel, a very successful teacher, joined the Christian Brothers because he felt he would have more opportunities to teach in a wider variety of schools and cities than those in the La Crosse and Marshfield, Wisconsin areas.

BROTHER DALE LENTZ - Lover of the land, lover of animals and lover of the outdoors describe Dale's growing up on a farm near North Washington, Iowa. He came to the Brothers of St. Pius X because they operated a farm, and he desired to work on a farm. He was the last appointed farm manager in Colby before the Brothers' Council decided to sell it in 1976. Brother Dale requested to leave the Congregation to purchase the farm. He did both, and because he had lost his father and his brother at the age of nineteen, he invited his mother and other family members to join him in Colby, where they still live to this day.

BROTHER STEVEN SIMS - This red-haired young man from La Crosse was blessed with musical talent and teaching skills, which he used very effectively for the ten years he was a Brother. When asked what he remembered about his time with the Congregation and what his legacy was, he mentioned that, being a small Community, the Brothers had opportunities for leadership, that all were encouraged to advance their spiritual knowledge by attending workshops and retreats in various places, and that the Brothers brought in different religious leaders for conferences. His gratitude for these experiences, which were shared by all, has traveled with him. Teaching at St. John's in Marshfield was the highlight of his career. The School Sisters of Notre Dame helped him to grow professionally and his involvement with parish life there as an organist was most rewarding.

Brother Steven Sims teaching at St. John's in Marshfield

In reflecting on the legacy he received from the Brothers, Brother Steven wrote the following: "The attendance at the reunions the Brothers of St. Pius X had these past ten years is a true testimony that we are still very much connected. Our Order did not die; it took on a new look. Many who shared in the life of the Brothers of St. Pius X still have a unique bond of true brotherhood. When we are together, it is like no time has passed. That is a true test. After Brother Gary left the Brothers of St. Pius X to become a Christian Brother, he continued to wear his Pius X final profession ring. He wore it proudly; and when those who asked what the ring represented, he told them. Shortly before his death, he asked me what memento I would like. I asked for his profession ring and made him the promise that I would wear it for the rest of my life. The ring is so meaningful to me. It is a constant reminder of my life as a Pius X Brother; it also sums up my true friendship with Brother Gary. In summary, to answer the question, *if you could turn the clock back to 1969, the year you entered, would you do this all over again,* my answer would be, without hesitation, a resounding, *Yes!*" This author thinks that many of the former Brothers would say the same.

Reunions

Early in 1999 it was decided that, in order to maintain contact with former members of the Community, a committee of Brother Charles, Brother Michael, Brother Gary Smith, FSC, Richard Berendes and Steven Sims was formed to plan a reunion. A plan was made to meet in La Crosse, invite Bishop Raymond Burke and all former members whose addresses were known, and to celebrate Mass and a meal together. Nineteen gathered to experience the spirit of the Brothers of St. Pius X again, as they had done in the past. Unbelievable to all was how close they felt to one another, and that the spirit of brotherhood continued, not only in those who remained Brothers of St. Pius X, but also, amazingly, in those who pursued other vocations in life. It was as though they were still united as one, which they were. The next day, Mass was held at Sacred Heart Church in De Soto, with Fathers Kevin Gordon, Eugene Katcher and John Beckfelt concelebrating. Thereafter, all toured the De Soto property which used to be the Brothers' monastery. This occasion led to planning the 50th anniversary celebration.

1999 Reunion in De Soto – above and below

First Row: Robert Klabunde, Fred Weber, Steven Sims, Brother Gary Smith

Second Row: Bishop Raymond L. Burke, Rev. John Beckfelt, Joseph Kubatska, Edward Zimmer, Francis Peters, Rev. Kevin Gordon

Third Row: James Althoff, Richard Berendes, Mark Resch, Donald McAllister, John Alvin, Rev. Eugene Katcher, Brother Charles Bisenius, Ronald Resong, Brother Michael Mandernach, John Nelson

In August of 2002, Bishop Burke was invited to be the celebrant at the Mass for the 50th anniversary of the Brotherhood. A Eucharistic celebration was planned at Holy Cross Diocesan Center. All the former Brothers were invited, as well as families and friends of the Brothers. Father Kevin Gordon gave a rousing homily to an overflowing crowd. Deacon Richard Sage and Earl Madary provided the music. Symbols (copies of the PAX, a habit, a profession ring, the Coat of Arms of Pope Pius X, and other items) were brought to the altar as part of the entrance procession. Members of the Place of Grace Catholic Worker House in La Crosse served a delicious dinner afterward. Father Michael Gorman, who had eight different Brothers as teachers of religious education at St. Philip's in Soldiers Grove, Mrs. Joan Peterson, Sister Marie Kyle, FSPA, and others spoke after the meal.

Reunion in Fargo, 2005; L to R – Brother Michael Mandernach, Fred Weber, Francis Peters, Richard Berendes, Ronald Resong, Brother Gary Smith, FSC., Donald McAllister, Brother Charles Bisenius and Steven Sims

Don and Jeanine McAllister invited the Brothers to come to their home in Fargo, North Dakota in 2005. Mass was celebrated, followed by a meal. They all toured Shanley High School and Saints Joachim and Anne Parish. The McAllisters own Hurley Religious Goods Store, so the group also delighted in all of the religious goods.

In 2008, a group of Brothers and former Brothers gathered in Cascade, Iowa at the home of Brother Charles to enjoy fellowship and celebrate Mass with Father John Beckfelt. The group joined the Trappist monks at New Mellerey for Vespers, toured the Basilica of St. Francis Xavier in Dyersville, Iowa, and shared a meal and picnic in Cascade. Their aim was to keep in touch, as well as to express their concern and care for each other.

2008 Reunion in Cascade, Iowa; L to R – Francis Peters, Brother Michael Mandernach, Brother Gary Smith, FSC., Richard Berendes, Brother Charles Bisenius, Father John Beckfelt, Arthur Roach, Joe Kubatska, Fred Weber, Donald McAllister and Brother Don Bosco McDermott

The 60th Reunion in 2012 was held in La Crosse at the home of Richard and Patricia Berendes. Again the Brothers had an outdoor picnic, after which they shared stories of their current lives and remembrances of their time together as Brothers. As part of the celebration, they prayed Compline, the night prayer of the Church. It seemed that each year, the sharing of deeper insights and experiences was drawing them closer as "Brothers" and as friends. They attended Mass on Sunday at the Shrine of our Lady of Guadalupe in La Crosse and shared in the brunch buffet there. They decided to finish the history of the Brothers within the next year and to meet again when the history was completed.

60th Reunion in La Crosse, Wisconsin in 2012; Standing L to R: Brother Michael Mandernach, Steven Sims, Robert Klabunde, Francis Peters, Thomas Keilen, Fred Weber, Joseph Kubatska and Richard Berendes; Seated are Marcus Resch and Donald McAllister

This narrative history of the Brothers of St. Pius X started with the beginning of *Psalm* 133: "How good and how delightful it is for all to live together as brothers." Throughout each day of our existence, we Brothers tried to live in harmony and peace. In living the consecrated life, we tried to witness to others and to each other as an image of what everlasting life would be in Heaven. This was what we Brothers were called to do. Therefore, it is fitting and right to close this writing with what God promises us all in the last verse of *Psalm* 133 (3b): "And the Lord pronounced His blessing, even life forevermore."

AFTERWORD

Brother Michael Mandernach

The Vatican II document *Decree on the Adaptation and Renewal of Religious Life (Perfectae Caritatis)* consistently emphasizes the primary importance of the renewal of the spiritual life. The main focus of the Brothers of St. Pius X was always the following of Jesus, as told in the Gospels. As Jesus called the Twelve to be His disciples, all men who came to be with us understood that living community life in brotherhood and following the Evangelical Counsels was our calling. Through the daily celebration of Mass and the chanting of the Divine Office, we prayed to God for the needs of the Church, the needs of people and the needs of our Community.

It was our desire that the strength of our prayer life and our dedication to our call as Brothers would reach out in ministry through the various works in our apostolate. Those works included being present to others through teaching, health care ministry, agriculture, candle making, arts and crafts and whatever other ministry to which we were called. To quote Bishop Treacy again, "Their works will be as broad as the Church."

Many questions have come to me while writing this history. How many lives, for instance, have the Brothers of St. Pius X touched through their ministry and presence these past sixty years? It is overwhelming to realize that, in the Diocese of La Crosse, we have ministered in over thirty parishes, ten grade and high schools and three health care institutions. In the Diocese of Superior, we have ministered in one parish and one health care facility. In the Archdiocese of Dubuque, we have ministered in twelve parishes and six schools. In the Archdiocese of Chicago, we have ministered in two high schools. In the Diocese of Erie, Pennsylvania we have ministered in one parish. Finally, in the Archdiocese of Detroit we have ministered in one health care center. We thank each of these institutions for giving us the opportunity to serve. Yes, we were few in number, but our outreach was far.

Even greater questions follow: What effect did the Brothers of St. Pius X have on the men who were with us and left? Did the nine men who became priests realize their calling to the priesthood because they were with us? Since I knew all nine of these men personally, lived with them, shared prayer with them and have met most of them many times since their ordinations, I have seen them as successful pastors, homilists and compassionate priests. What a gift to the Church they have been!

Were the vocations of the men who became husbands and fathers enriched because they shared communal living, sometimes had to cook and clean, and because they shared in the celebration of the Mass and prayer? When I see these men with their wives, I sense a radiating love that exists between them. I see how they respect their wives and love their children. They tell of their faithfulness to God and to the Church. I pray that their being with us has helped them in their calling.

Were the men who chose to remain single helped by their time with us? I sense that some continued somewhat the same style of prayer and dedication to God as they did when they were with us. One former Brother, an organist, today plays for all three Sunday Masses in his parish. One who is single takes care of his mother and other members of his family.

Were the Brothers who joined other religious communities well-prepared to assume membership in those Congregations? I know that they received a sound formation in spirituality and religious life with the Brothers of St. Pius X. Academically they received an education in their chosen career that was more than satisfactory. I know that all of them were a positive addition to their new Congregations.

I regret that we did not keep in contact with all the members. I certainly have not forgotten them. I know that many of those who left have since died. May God grant them eternal rest.

AFTERWORD

Richard Berendes

The Community of the Brothers of St. Pius X was called into being at a unique time in the life of the Church and the world in general. The world stage had seen the formation of the British Commonwealth, the United Nations, and the devastation of the World War II. It had seen the beginning of the advancement of human rights in the United States on the one hand and the simultaneous assassination of multiple leaders on the other. The mid to late 1950's saw the birth of rock-n-roll and the early 1960's ushered in the so-called sexual revolution. The new Community of Brothers, at the same time, was struggling to find its way and place in a changing Church and society.

At the same time, the Church was struggling to find its way in a complex and increasingly secular world. A major theme of the Second Vatican Council that had a huge impact on the new Community was the role of the Church in the modern world, which included liturgical reform, reforms started by Pope Pius X, advanced by Pope Pius XII and expanded by Vatican II. Also addressed was the role of the laity which would have an impact throughout the whole Church, but were experienced here in this rural diocese. The "Church in the Modern World" called for restored attention to the dignity of the person. It called for attention to human and economic justice in civil society that ensured the dignified treatment of its citizens. Special attention was given to those parts of the world which lacked or experienced denied access to the Gospel and basic human rights and freedoms. The new Community of Brothers, as a small, young, energetic and poor Community, were well-positioned in rural, economically-deprived areas to witness and to catechize during the changing expression of the Church, especially around the Liturgy of the Eucharist.

Several recurring questions arose in exploring my history as a Brother of St. Pius X. The first would be: What was the purpose for founding the group? This would include an understanding of the vision of the founder, Bishop Treacy, and the Community's own shared understanding of its purpose.

The second question regarded the financial standing of the Community. The group learned that it would have to be totally self-supporting within the first few months of its existence. Practically speaking then, the Community was to be self-sufficient in a ministry "as broad as the Church."

Finally, in reviewing the history and my experience as a Brother, a third question arises regarding the acceptance and support of the Community by the Church of the Diocese of La Crosse. Given the changes occurring within the Church and society locally, nationally and internationally, there seemed to be room for the existence of a new community of religious men within the Diocese. Perhaps the more appropriate challenge to raise is: Were the Brothers a consistent part of the choir of voices inviting the faithful to a new expression of Church and, central to that, its sacred worship?

The ultimate question remains: What gifts did the Community of the Brothers bring in their short history? That answer lies in the experience of the men who served as Brothers as well as with the people they served. I would offer that the Brothers, for a short time in the history of the rural Diocese of La Crosse, served as a bridge connecting the Church of the 1950's with reforms promulgated by the Second Vatican Council. A Brother is the perfect companion for the struggles of turbulent times like these; he is someone to walk with, to talk with, to pray with, and in so doing share life with. So we remain *Together as Brothers*.

Working on 'Together As Brothers' at the Holy Cross Diocesan Center
L to R: Richard Berendes, Rose Peterson and Brother Michael Mandernach

AFTERWORD

Rose Peterson

Serendipity: luck that takes the form of finding valuable or pleasant things that are not looked for; a fortuitous happenstance or pleasant surprise. This word perfectly describes my involvement with this book project and the Brothers of St. Pius X.

I first met Richard Berendes when he was a Brother and an LPN at St. Francis Hospital. I was 18 and a Nursing Assistant at St. Francis. Over the years our paths crossed again, as our nursing careers and lives evolved. When Richard (now more commonly called Dick) retired in 2009 I got to know him and his wife, Pat, better. In the summer of 2012, they invited me to help them host the 60th Reunion of the Brothers of St. Pius X. I have to admit I had no idea who St. Pius X was, and the only Brothers I knew from that group were Brother Richard and Brother Kevin (Gordon), who also worked at St. Francis in the Inhalation Therapy Department. Although I knew they had some kind of religious connection, I had no idea what they were all about. Helping to host that summer reunion event at the Berendes' was about to change all that! What a wonderful and powerful experience it was to be part of their group for the weekend!

I met Brother Michael Mandernach for the first time at this reunion, as well as all of the former Brothers, many who came with their wives, who traveled quite a distance to reconvene. I was surprised at how close these men were, regardless of the path their lives took. Conversation came easily and when they shared prayer it was magical and mystical. It was as if time and distance only strengthened the bond that held these men together. I couldn't help but wonder if it was this strong 60 years later, how strong it must have been when they were together as Brothers! I came away from that weekend knowing I had witnessed something special.

In January 2013, when Brother Michael came to the Holy Cross Diocesan Center in La Crosse to write the book, I again met him. We shared a meal and I learned about his writing and that he was correcting edits done by Monsignor Malnar. I offered to help with those (as Monsignor Malnar offered many changes!). And so began my involvement with the book! What started as simple editing has turned into formatting and so much more. I now know what self-publishing means, from purchasing an ISBN number, to learning the correct definitions (and spelling) for Foreword, Afterword and Preface, along with the correct usage of numerals and punctuation.

We have been blessed with good proof-readers that have offered correct theological content and improved the writing and flow of the book – several times over! Brother Michael, Dick, and I have spent many an evening at the Diocesan Center – Brother Michael with one set of edits, and Dick with the other, while I typed what they dictated. And then there was the reward of a drink (a manhattan for the men of course!) afterward at South Lanes or Fiesta Mexicana, and perhaps a meal prior to working at either Houghtons or Hungry Peddler. What a long process this has been – but wonderful, awe-inspiring, mind-expanding, sad, and joyful all at the same time!

As I listen to Brother Michael and read his writing, I have a better picture of what these men were and continue to be about. I understand their commitment – to God, to each other, and to community – regardless of the whether they chose a single or married path or the priesthood.

We learn how small our world really is as life unfolds. In Fall of 2012, my youngest son, Zachary, ventured off to Ashland to attend Northland College. Dick has been a wonderful mentor and support for Zach, and accompanied us when Zach moved into the dorm. While we were up there, we visited Father Kevin Gordon (formerly Brother Kevin), who lives in Bayfield and ministers to five different parishes in the area. We had a meal together, which has turned into a visit with him every time we travel north, and he has been gracious in storing Zach's refrigerator and t. v. so we don't have to haul it back and forth each year.

There is only one word for my experience in meeting these men and writing this book – serendipity! Every part of it has been a pleasant surprise – with every experience connecting to the next one. Meeting these men for the first time in 2012, and learning and writing about them as young Brothers has provided me with a clear picture of what a Brother is; I understand calling, commitment, and lived-discipleship. What a fortuitous happenstance!

Recollection of the Life of a Brother in Art

Brother Martin (John) McTarsney, a member of our community for nearly seven years from 1957 through 1962, recalled his life with the

Brothers in art on August 4, 1973, from 2:00 a.m. to 4:00 a.m. This unique piece of artwork reflects his time with us; every member will be able to recall many of the same events and places. A magnifying glass may help to see the images more clearly.

St. Anne's Chapel is top center with statues of the Blessed Virgin Mary and St. Joseph to the sides and the PAX symbol on the front of the altar. Going clockwise, to the right of the chapel is our main house with Sacred Heart Church in the background. Below the main house appear beehives with a jar of honey. Below that, you will see a train, a plane, Lansing Bridge, the Mississippi River and the beautiful bluffs along the River.

He lists the members of his class: Brothers Martin, Paul, Claude and Simon. A meat grinder tells of the butchering of our own meat, and the loaf of bread of our baking and cooking. To the left you will see the vestment cabinet and a toboggan. November 9, 1957 is his day of entrance.

Continuing clockwise is a Bishop with a crosier and the simplicity of a Brother's bedroom. On the bottom is our habit, a journal and a coat of arms. E.P. and A.R. stand for Fathers Edward Penchi and Albert Roemer, our directors. Clockwise is Brother Martin sitting in a choir stall with the word Magnificat and the cities where he taught catechetics. Notice the clothes on the clothesline and issues of THE PAX flying out of the printers. Each day the Brothers walked from the chapel to the dining room and also walked up to the top of the bluffs.

This drawing reveals what was important to us: our chapel with our prayer life, our sharing of community life with one another, our ministries in our apostolate, our small monastery on the banks of the Mississippi River, the people who came to visit us and the good people of the De Soto area.

Addendum A

CANDIDATES

The following is a list of the candidates of the Brothers of St. Pius X and each man's year of entrance. A few who stayed a short period of time are not included in this list. Those whose names do not include a "Name as Brother" were not invested with the habit. Those with an asterisk after their name we know to be deceased.

NAME	NAME AS BROTHER	HOME CITY
1952		
Donald McAllister	Thomas	Wausau, Wisconsin
Marcus Resch	John	Wausau, Wisconsin
William Kundert	Joseph	Arpin, Wisconsin
Francis Peters	Francis	West Bend, Wisconsin
Wilfred Mandernach	Michael	St. Martin, Minnesota
Don Bosco McDermott*	Don Bosco	Bernard, Iowa
Ralph Gianoli*	Anthony	Genoa, Wisconsin
Charles Bisenius*	Charles	Cascade, Iowa
James Althoff*		Earlville, Iowa
1953		
George Bellman	Mark	Bremerton, Washington
Francis Higgins*	Martin	Winthrop, Iowa
Alfred Amorino		Oakland, California
John Debis*	Francis	New York, New York
Edward Zimmer*	Edward	Spring Valley, Wisconsin

1954

Richard Delaney*	Richard	Peoria, Illinois
Otto Hommerding*	Joseph	Wausau, Wisconsin
George Cormier	Philip	Gardner, Massachusetts

1955

William Callari*	Stephen	Escanaba, Michigan
James Riley	Ignatius	Ashland, Wisconsin
John Benware	Paul	Holland, Michigan
James Donnan	James	Dubuque, Iowa
Donald Scott		Columbus, Ohio

1956

John Nelson*	Dominic	Rochester, Minnesota
Melvin Welbes*	Joachim	Wausau, Wisconsin
Casimir Drzewiecki	Casimir	Toledo, Ohio
James Lynch	Joseph	Wichita, Kansas
William Ryan	William Robert	New York, New York
Joseph Green	Aquinas	St. Louis, Missouri
James Henry	Peter Thomas	Norwood, Massachusetts
John Alvin*	Jude	Richland Center, Wisconsin
Milo Duellman*	Cletus	Fountain City, Wisconsin
John Beckfelt	Alcuin	Grand Rapids, Minnesota

1957

Jerome Krieg		Mosinee, Wisconsin
Richard Jira*	Augustine	Sioux Falls, South Dakota
Bernard Wavrunek*	Bernard	Neillsville, Wisconsin

1958

John McTarsney*	Martin	Staten Island, New York
Arthur Roach	Paul	Eau Claire, Wisconsin
Roger Krentz	Simon	Princeton, Wisconsin
William Eddy	Claude	Waterbury, Connecticut

1959

Michael Tierney	James	Independence, Missouri
Ronald Resong	Francis	Neillsville, Wisconsin
Robert Lynch	Ignatius	Chicago, Illinois
Thomas Heber	Matthew	Harvey, North Dakota
James McGinley	Kevin	Gays Mills, Wisconsin
Albert Mozgis		Aurora, Illinois
Wesley Hayes		Brooklyn, New York
John Jones		Newton, Iowa
Herbert Schmidt	Raphael	Fort Atkinson, Wisconsin
Wesley Hickie*	John	Worcester, Massachusetts

1960

| Arturo Peralto* | Xavier | Albuquerque, New Mexico |

Forrest Viet	Nicholas	New York, New York
Keith Andersen*	Adrian	Green Bay, Wisconsin
Jay Henninger	Conrad	Minneapolis, Minnesota
Michael Hansen	Joseph	La Crosse, Wisconsin

1961

Fred Weber	Joseph	Mondovi, Wisconsin
Walter Gray		La Crosse, Wisconsin
Eugene Gentile		Hurley, Wisconsin
William Brown		Baltimore, Maryland
James Hornback		New Haven, Kentucky

1962

Gerard Schulte	Gerard	Schererville, Indiana
George Griller	David	Sioux Falls, South Dakota

1963

Arthur Brutcher	Kevin	Buffalo, New York
Joseph Kubatska*	Gerald	Buffalo, Iowa
Arthur Christensen	Carlos	Owatonna, Minnesota
Anthony Sustarich		White Pines, Michigan
Leland Buchta		Beaver Dam, Wisconsin
Kenneth Prusik	Andre	Shawano, Wisconsin
Louis Mullen	Fabian	Dougherty, Iowa
Nicholas Shepherd		Michigan City, Indiana

Kenneth Lucas*	Paul	Watertown, New York

1964

Kevin Gordon	Kevin	Bayfield, Wisconsin
John Steuck	John	Rudolph, Wisconsin
John Logan		Philadelphia, Pennsylvania
Daniel Kohler	Daniel	Tonawanda, New York
Thomas Keilen	Thomas	New Richmond, Wisconsin
Carl Burger		Worthington, Iowa
Thomas Brinkman		Appleton, Wisconsin

1965

Gary Smith*	Gary	Cincinnati, Ohio
James Pultz	James	Pavilion, New York
Richard Berendes	Richard	Norwalk, Wisconsin
Eugene Katcher	Eugene	Detroit, Michigan
Michael Neary*	Michael	Spring Lake, Minnesota
Thomas Maikowski	Thomas	Milwaukee, Wisconsin
Fred Murray		Shreveport, Louisiana
Francis Stone		Philadelphia, Pennsylvania

1966

Michael Smith	Michael	Menomonee, Michigan
Robert Grams	Robert	St. Cloud, Minnesota
Robert Klabunde	Robert	Wauwatosa, Wisconsin

Joseph Sharp		Springfield, Ohio
Peter Marzen		Stacyville, Iowa

1967

Francis Nitkowski		Portsmouth, New Hampshire
Patrick Pisarek		Necedah, Wisconsin
Louis Jennewein		Patchogue, New York
Robert Julian		Southbridge, Massachusetts

1968

George Viellieux		Somerset, Wisconsin
Daniel Landowski	Daniel	Milwaukee, Wisconsin
Dale Lentz	Dale	North Washington, Iowa

1969

Richard Casola		Rockford, Illinois
David Leos		Carlsbad, New Mexico
Steven Sims	Steven	La Crosse, Wisconsin
John Wech	John	Lincoln Park, Michigan

1971

Ronald Wendl		Elkader, Iowa

1972

Wayne Truckey*		Stiles, Wisconsin

1975

Richard Lerche		Milwaukee, Wisconsin

Addendum B

PARISHES, SCHOOLS and INSTITUTIONS where BROTHERS of ST. PIUS X TAUGHT, MINISTERED or WORKED from 1952 to 2013

DIOCESE OF LA CROSSE, WISCONSIN

St. Bernard's Parish, Abbotsford

St. Kilian's Parish, Bear Valley

St. Luke's Parish, Boyceville

St. Anthony de Padua School and Parish, Cazenovia

St. Mary's School, Colby

Sacred Heart Parish, De Soto

St. Wenceslaus Parish, Eastman

St. Mary's Parish, Galesville

St. Mary's Parish, Gays Mills

St. Charles Borromeo Parish, Genoa

Nativity of the Blessed Virgin Mary Parish, Keyesville

St. Pius X Parish and School, La Crosse

St. Thomas More School, La Crosse

St. James School, La Crosse

Aquinas High School, La Crosse

Roncalli Newman Center, La Crosse

St. Francis Hospital, La Crosse

St. Michael's Home, La Crosse

Holy Cross Seminary, La Crosse

La Crosse Halfway Federation, La Crosse

Catholic Cemeteries, La Crosse

Sacred Heart Parish, Lone Rock

Columbus High School, Marshfield

Our Lady of Peace School, Marshfield

St. John the Baptist Parish and School, Marshfield

Sacred Heart School, Marshfield

St. Joseph's Hospital, Marshfield

St. Thomas Parish, Milan

St. Mary's Parish, Neillsville

St. Michael's Parish, North Creek

St. Patrick's Parish, Onalaska

St. John Nepomucene Parish and School, Prairie du Chien

St. James Parish, Rising Sun

St. Philip's Parish, Rolling Ground

St. Patrick's Parish, Seneca

Christ the King Parish, Spencer

Pacelli High School, Stevens Point

Sacred Heart Parish, Spring Valley

St. Bernard/St. Hedwig Schools, Thorp

St. Mary's Parish, Tomah

St. Bartholomew Parish, Trempealeau

St. Andrew Parish, Warrens

Sacred Heart Parish, Wauzeka

St. John the Baptist Parish, Wuerzburg

DIOCESE OF SUPERIOR, WISCONSIN

Sacred Heart Parish, Stetsonville

Marshfield Clinic, Ladysmith

ARCHDIOCESE OF DUBUQUE, IOWA

St. Patrick School, Anamosa

St. Mary's Parish, Dorchester

St. Francis Parish, Fayette

St. Mary's Parish, Hanover

St. Francis Xavier Parish, Hawkeye

Regis High School, Cedar Rapids

St. Pius X School, Cedar Rapids

St. Matthew School, Cedar Rapids

All Saints School, Cedar Rapids

St. Patrick School, Epworth

Immaculate Conception Parish, Lansing

St. George High School, Lansing

St. Joseph School, Farley

St. John School, Peosta

St. Joseph School, Marian

Sacred Heart School, Maquoketa

Sacred Heart School, Monticello

St. Mary's Parish, McGregor

St. John School of Religion, New Hampton

Immaculate Conception Parish, Wexford

Sacred Heart Parish, Volga

St. Joseph Parish, Wadena

St. Luke's School, St. Lucas

ARCHDIOCESE OF CHICAGO, ILLINOIS

St. Joseph High School, Westchester

Notre Dame High School, Niles

ARCHDIOCESE OF DETROIT, MICHIGAN

Detroit Memorial Hospital, Detroit

DIOCESE OF ERIE, PENNSYLVANIA

St. Teresa of Avila Parish, Union City

Prayer of St. Pius X

O Holy Father, Pius X,
saintly pastor ascended to the glory
of the Blessed, hear the prayer which
we lay at your feet. Obtain for us the
true love of Jesus, so that we may
live only in him. Grant us your great
devotion to the Virgin Mary. Deliver us
from every evil of soul and body.
And obtain that the church and all
Christianity may - as you so ardently
desire - sing the hymn of victory
and of peace.
Amen